PET TREATS AND PROCESSED CHICKEN FROM CHINA: CONCERNS FOR AMERICAN CONSUMERS AND PETS

HEARING

BEFORE THE

CONGRESSIONAL-EXECUTIVE COMMISSION ON CHINA

ONE HUNDRED THIRTEENTH CONGRESS

SECOND SESSION

JUNE 17, 2014

Printed for the use of the Congressional-Executive Commission on China

Available via the World Wide Web: http://www.cecc.gov

U.S. GOVERNMENT PUBLISHING OFFICE

88–496 PDF   WASHINGTON : 2015

For sale by the Superintendent of Documents, U.S. Government Publishing Office
Internet: bookstore.gpo.gov   Phone: toll free (866) 512–1800; DC area (202) 512–1800
Fax: (202) 512–2104   Mail: Stop IDCC, Washington, DC 20402–0001

CONGRESSIONAL-EXECUTIVE COMMISSION ON CHINA

LEGISLATIVE BRANCH COMMISSIONERS

Senate

SHERROD BROWN, Ohio, *Chairman*
CARL LEVIN, Michigan
DIANNE FEINSTEIN, California
JEFF MERKLEY, Oregon

House

CHRIS SMITH, New Jersey, *Cochairman*
FRANK WOLF, Virginia
ROBERT PITTENGER, North Carolina
MARK MEADOWS, North Carolina
TIM WALZ, Minnesota
MARCY KAPTUR, Ohio
MICHAEL HONDA, California

EXECUTIVE BRANCH COMMISSIONERS

NISHA DESAI BISWAL, U.S. Department of State

LAWRENCE T. LIU, *Staff Director*
PAUL B. PROTIC, *Deputy Staff Director*

(II)

CONTENTS

STATEMENTS

Page

APPENDIX

PREPARED STATEMENTS

SUBMISSION FOR THE RECORD

QUESTIONS AND ANSWERS FOR THE RECORD

PET TREATS AND PROCESSED CHICKEN FROM CHINA: CONCERNS FOR AMERICAN CONSUMERS AND PETS

CONGRESSIONAL-EXECUTIVE
COMMISSION ON CHINA,
Washington, DC.

The hearing was convened, pursuant to notice, at 3:38 p.m., in room 562 Dirksen Senate Office Building, Senator Sherrod Brown, Chairman, presiding.

Also present: Representative Christopher Smith.

OPENING STATEMENT OF HON. SHERROD BROWN, A U.S. SENATOR FROM OHIO; CHAIRMAN, CONGRESSIONAL–EXECUTIVE COMMISSION ON CHINA

Chairman BROWN. I call this hearing to order.

Thank you, Mr. Engeljohn, Ms. Forfa. I will introduce you in a moment. Thank you for joining us. I thank my Cochair, Congressman Smith, for being here and for his interest always in these issues that are important to our country on so many different levels.

I'll do a brief opening statement and turn it to Congressman Smith, then we will proceed with the witnesses.

I called this hearing to seek answers for American consumers, pet owners, farmers, and parents about the safety of pet treats and processed chicken and animal feed from the People's Republic of China. Americans want to know where their food comes from and want to make sure that everything is being done to keep it safe.

Sixty-two million households in this country have a pet. We raise 83 million dogs, 96 million cats. Many of us raise our animals almost like members of our families. That's why it's so troubling that we still do not know, seven years in, if you will, what's causing the deaths and illnesses of thousands of dogs.

Just last month, the U.S. Food and Drug Administration [FDA] said the reports of illnesses had increased to 5,600 pets, including 1,000 dog deaths and now 3 human illnesses. While no cause has been identified despite extensive studies, the illnesses may be linked to pet treats from China.

Days later, major pet stores, Petco and PetSmart, announced they would be phasing out the sale of pet treats from China because of safety concerns they have and their customers have. Many of us remember the pet food scare and recalls of 2007, a result of melamine-tainted pet food from China.

Given this, pet owners in Ohio and across America are rightfully concerned when they go to the store to buy treats and food for their pet. They face a difficult and confusing question, just like the ones our family faces for our dog, Franklin. If something says it's made in China, can we be assured that it's safe? If it says "Made in the USA," what exactly does that mean? Is everything being done to keep pet treats safe?

Last year, the U.S. Department of Agriculture [USDA] declared that China is eligible to export processed cooked chicken to the United States, paving the way for chicken sourced in the United States to be shipped to China for processing and sold back to American consumers.

While no chicken has entered our shores yet, it's possible that very soon this processed chicken could end up on our dinner tables and in our school lunchrooms. Can we just trust our Chinese counterparts to enforce safety up to our own standards given China's poor enforcement of their own laws and rampant corruption?

We know what we have learned over the last 100 years in our country, to rely on the regulatory system to produce safe food, safe drinking water, clean air, all other kinds of safe ingredients in our pharmaceutical system because we know that the role of government and consumer protection is so important and Americans by and large trust their government to do that. Will the label clearly indicate that the chicken was processed in China in some cases so Americans can make an informed choice?

Finally, researchers are exploring a possible link between animal feed from China and the PEDv virus that has wiped out some 10 percent of our pig population. It's been a year and no definitive cause has been identified. Americans want and require better answers and clearer labels and the peace of mind that the foods we import from China are safe.

I appreciate the FDA and USDA being here to shed more light on these issues to help American consumers better understand them. In the meantime, I urge the Chinese Government to fully cooperate with our agencies and to make significant improvements in their food safety system.

I urge our FDA and USDA to continue devoting every effort in determining the cause of the pet illnesses and PEDv. I urge companies to ensure the highest safety standards and to put pet and human safety first. Finally, I would urge us in Congress to consider whether we need to update our own labeling requirements to take into account an increasingly globalized marketplace and supply chain and to ensure the public health of our citizens.

Congressman Smith, welcome.

STATEMENT OF HON. CHRISTOPHER SMITH, A U.S. REPRESENTATIVE FROM NEW JERSEY; COCHAIRMAN, CONGRESSIONAL–EXECUTIVE COMMISSION ON CHINA

Representative SMITH. Thank you very much, Chairman Brown. Thank you for calling this important hearing. I want to welcome our distinguished witnesses to this hearing on the important issue of the safety of our food products from China.

This is the second hearing on food safety that the Commission has done in the past year, and I especially want to thank Chairman Brown and our very dedicated and professional staff for their work to raise awareness about this issue, as well as all other human rights, rule of law, and governance issues.

The safety of food, feed, and drugs from China is a cause of real concern. American consumers are rightly anxious. We have pet treats that may have sickened and/or killed many pets across America. A virus may decimate 10 percent of American pigs, possibly from vitamins or feed from China. We have food products, including processed chicken, that may not have labeled as being made in China. In fact, it may have been labeled ''Made in America.''

I want to thank Chris D'Urso for bringing this last issue to my attention. The maze of labels and labeling requirements called ''Country of Origin Labeling'' [COOL] makes it difficult for American consumers to make reasoned choices about the foods they eat and those foods that they feed to their pets.

Christopher D'Urso is one of the most outstanding young men that I have encountered. Not only did he achieve a perfect SAT score and ranked number one in his class, but his record of public service at such a young age is extraordinarily rare.

Last year we met and he brought information to me and to my staff, and to the Commission staff, about his research and findings regarding Origin of Labeling laws for the United States. The thoroughness and the level of understanding in such a complex and international issue was indeed impressive.

Having researched this issue since 2012, he pointed to the inadequacies of many of our current laws. In fact, consumers have the right to know the country of origin of products, especially when they eat those products. I believe his future contributions will be significant.

On the issue of food safety, both Chinese and American consumers share serious concerns about food products made in China. I know I look, but again, we don't always know that what we're looking at is actually the truth. We really hope there can be more cooperation, accountability, and transparency in the future.

This past week was Food Safety Awareness Week in China. China's food industry has faced a real crisis of confidence over the past seven years. Despite government efforts, the number of scandals continue to grow: Meat that glows in the dark; exploding watermelons; 40 tons of bean sprouts containing antibiotics; rice contaminated with heavy metals; mushrooms soaked with bleach; and pork so filled with stimulants that athletes were told not to eat them, because they would test positive for banned substances. All on top of the melamine-tainted milk powder that sickened some 300,000 children in 2007. As we all know, the World Health Organization [WHO] has said that melamine can cause kidney failure, bladder and kidney stones, and even may be a carcinogen.

In response to that scandal, China passed its first ever food safety law. Nevertheless, we all know well that there is often a gap between what Chinese law says and what is enforced. China is still struggling to keep its food supply healthy.

The Chinese Government is trying to crack down, we are told, recently closing some 5,000 food-producing businesses and arresting over 2,000 people. But experts on food safety say a needlessly complex bureaucracy and fierce determination to turn a profit means there will continue to be food safety scares and a Chinese public wary about its own supply.

While we think that this issue would have been solved already if China transferred resources to food safety from censoring the Internet and cracking down on free speech and political dissent. Unfortunately, the government still seems to want safe pork but a silent public.

There is a direct connection between better human rights conditions in China and food safety. While China has had unprecedented economic growth for decades, it lags behind in ensuring the rights of its citizens and in developing transparency, official accountability and rule of law, things it certainly needs to tackle like the issue of food safety.

Transparency is absolutely necessary for any government to protect the health and well-being of citizens and to effectively manage problems related to food and drug safety. Remember the secrecy about the SAARS? Free speech and free press and freedom of association would allow crusading journalists in civil society to expose health scandals and work toward open solutions.

Those who try to skirt the law for profit would be exposed and citizens could work together with their government to ensure better and healthier food and water. A free press and muckraking journalists and novelists like Upton Sinclair—who we all recall wrote ''The Jungle'' about unsanitary meat, and it led to the Pure Food and Drug Act of 1906, that eventually morphed through legislation into the FDA—certainly helped to bring better food safety to the United States.

It may be tempting to say that China is on a learning curve that will eventually produce better food safety. But they need journalists, they need people who can speak out, use the Internet, and expose what is happening.

Let me conclude by saying U.S. trade policy must put health and safety of U.S. consumers and their pets as its top priority. Safety before profits is the message that has to be sent to producers, processors, and manufacturers.

If U.S. inspections are blocked or delayed for any reason, we should consider swiftly pulling products from shelves. In addition, the United States must tell authorities in China that they are held accountable for implementing and enforcing laws on food and drug safety.

The United States should be negotiating as part of its diplomatic relations better and smarter inspections, again, transparency in the food and drug supply chain, and closer collaboration between our food safety experts. Our labeling of food and feed products must be clear so that consumers know what they are buying and from whom, and where it comes from.

Last, the United States must continue to make human rights a top priority of U.S.-China relations, free speech, and an active civil society will do much more to ensure safer food and expose corruption.

I yield back, and I thank you.

Chairman BROWN. Thank you, Congressman Smith.

Dr. Daniel Engeljohn is the Assistant Administrator at the Food Safety and Inspection Service, Office of Field Operations, U.S. Department of Agriculture, responsible for oversight of the risk management policies for food safety and animal welfare conducted by nearly 7,800 employees and approximately 6,000 meat and poultry processing and import facilities. He served as scientific spokesperson on food safety strategies. Dr. Engeljohn, welcome.

Tracy Forfa is the Deputy Director of the Center for Veterinary Medicine at the Food and Drug Administration. The center regulates the manufacture and distribution of drugs and food additives given to animals, both food derived and companion. She's been with the Center for Veterinary Medicine since 2002. Prior to her appointment, she helped support FDA's mission for working on external dispute resolution to blood banking.

She is a graduate of Wooster College, just 30 miles from where I grew up. Ms. Forfa, thank you for joining us.

Dr. Engeljohn, if you would present your testimony. Thank you.

STATEMENT OF DANIEL L. ENGELJOHN, PH.D., ASSISTANT ADMINISTRATOR, OFFICE OF FIELD OPERATIONS, FOOD SAFETY AND INSPECTION SERVICE, U.S. DEPARTMENT OF AGRICULTURE

Mr. ENGELJOHN. Thank you, Chairman Brown and Cochairman Smith, members of the Commission. I am Dr. Daniel Engeljohn with the USDA's Food Safety Inspection Service [FSIS], Office of Field Operations. I am pleased to appear before you today to explain the current state of U.S. regulatory oversight of poultry exported from the People's Republic of China for human food.

Let me take some time to explain FSIS's mandate. By law, FSIS is required to examine and inspect all slaughtered and processed livestock and poultry, as well as all processed egg products produced for use in commerce for human consumption.

Our inspectors and veterinarians monitor the health of the animals brought to slaughter and ensure that livestock are treated humanely. They are also responsible for collecting the samples that our scientists analyze for the presence of pathogens and illegal drug residues.

These dedicated men and women are on the front lines nationwide, ensuring that the regulations and directives are backed by scientific evidence to ensure that meat, poultry, and processed egg products in commerce are safe and wholesome.

FSIS also regulates all imported meat, poultry, and processed egg products intended for use as human food through a three-step process. First, before FSIS-regulated products can enter the country, the agency determines whether the food safety regulatory system of any country that wishes to export to the United States is equivalent to our own inspection system. Second, once FSIS finds a foreign system to be equivalent, FSIS then re-inspects eligible product from that country at U.S. points of entry.

During fiscal year 2013, FSIS personnel inspected approximately 3 billion pounds of meat and poultry products presented for import from 28 actively exporting foreign countries, as well as about 10 million pounds of processed egg products. Third, FSIS evaluates an exporting country's food safety system on an ongoing basis. Each year, FSIS reviews any changes in the foreign country's food safety system.

Let me now explain, briefly, where we are in the process for China, a process that began in 2004 and, with their request for onsite FSIS audits, we began the process for looking at poultry processing and slaughter in their system.

First, the United States is not importing any chicken that was slaughtered in China. The March 2013 audit by FSIS found that China's poultry slaughter system was not equivalent to that of the United States.

Then second, FSIS reaffirmed in August 2013 that China's poultry processing inspection system is equivalent to that in the United States. This means that chickens slaughtered here in the United States or in another country whose poultry system is equivalent to that in the United States could be sent to China for processing and then re-exported to the United States.

The only chicken currently permitted to be imported from China is processed chicken from approved sources. FSIS, in coordination with USDA's Animal and Plant Health Inspection Service [APHIS], also currently requires that all processed chicken products from China be fully cooked.

China has provided a list of four plants it has certified as eligible to export processed chicken to the United States. However, before any processed chicken can be exported to the United States, a proper export health certificate must be developed by China and approved by FSIS and APHIS.

This certificate must demonstrate that the poultry is sourced from the United States or from another country that has an equivalent system as in the United States, and then must also certify that the poultry was cooked to a proper temperature, among other things.

We received a draft of this certificate earlier this month and, when it is approved, China will then be able to determine when to begin shipping products from plants certified to export processed poultry to the United States.

The agency does not have any information about how much processed poultry, if any, is expected to ship from China once certification is up and running. In addition to carrying out a proper certificate, a product must be properly labeled.

We are well aware of the consumer concerns regarding this matter. Under Title 9 of the Code of Federal Regulations, immediate containers of poultry products imported into the United States must bear labels showing the name of the country of origin.

Because processed poultry product from China must be cooked, FSIS believes that it is unlikely that the product would be repacked or further processed in this country, therefore, we believe that consumers would likely be able to determine from the label that they are purchasing product from China.

If the product were to be repacked or further processed in the United States, it would not include information that such product was from China but it would be repacked or processed under FSIS inspection.

The dedicated men and women of FSIS work every day for a common and extremely important goal of preventing food-borne illness. We take our mission seriously and understand the important role of ensuring the safety of the nation's food supply, whether domestic or from foreign establishments.

Thank you for your continued support and the opportunity to report on the work we do to protect public health.

Chairman BROWN. Thank you, Dr. Engeljohn.

Ms. Forfa, welcome.

STATEMENT OF TRACEY FORFA, J.D., DEPUTY DIRECTOR, CENTER FOR VETERINARY MEDICINE, U.S. FOOD AND DRUG ADMINISTRATION

Ms. FORFA. Good afternoon, again. Chairman Brown, Cochairman Smith, thank you. I am Tracey Forfa, Deputy Director of the Center for Veterinary Medicine at the Food and Drug Administration [FDA], and I really appreciate the opportunity to be here today to update you on FDA's investigation into reported illnesses in pets that have consumed jerky pet treats.

As of last month, we had received approximately 4,800 such reports, including 1,800 since we did an update in October of last year. The reports received involved illnesses in more than 5,600 dogs, 24 cats, 3 humans, and sadly, involved more than 1,000 canine deaths. Most of the reported cases involved chicken, duck, or sweet potato jerky products imported from China.

Unfortunately, to date FDA has not been able to identify a specific cause for the reported illnesses or deaths, despite an intensive scientific investigation. Getting to the bottom of this problem is definitely a priority for FDA and the agency is continuing its comprehensive investigation.

This ongoing global investigation is complex and involves a wide variety of experts. We have collaborated with our colleagues in academia and industry, and have reached out to the pet firms in the United States to enlist their help and share data with them.

We are updating veterinarians and pet owners as we receive information on our Web site, and we have a Web page dedicated specifically to issues related to jerky pet treats.

Our last major update, as you know, was last month. This information has been further disseminated to veterinarians by various groups, including the American Veterinary Medical Association.

The 4,800 reports that we have received cover many sizes and ages of dogs and include multiple breeds. About 60 percent of the reports we receive are for gastrointestinal illnesses and about 30 percent relate to kidney or urinary issues. The remaining 10 percent of cases involve a variety of other symptoms, including convulsions, tremors, hives, and skin irritation.

We had a surge of complaints after we published, in October of last year, an update. The agency has determined that about 25 percent of those 1,800 cases were historic, which means illnesses occurred several months or even years previously. The remaining cases were more recent, but may or may not have received veterinary attention.

Of the new cases that we have received since October, we have identified about 125 well-documented cases which we are further investigating. We continue to correspond with owners and veterinarians of these pets to track their progress and obtain test samples when they're available.

We also are working with state and university diagnostic laboratories to collect 250 jerky treat samples that are connected to consumer-related complaints, plus more than 200 retail samples that we've obtained on our own, and we've performed more than 1,000 tests on these samples.

This has included intensive testing for numerous contaminants, as well as examining composition of jerky pet treats to verify that they actually do contain the ingredients listed on the label and do not contain ingredients that are not listed.

In addition to this work, we have held regular meetings with the Chinese Administration of Quality, Supervision, Inspection, and Quarantine [AQSIQ] about the jerky pet treat issue.

In April 2012, we conducted inspections of several facilities in China that manufacture jerky pet treats for export. We selected these firms specifically because the jerky products they manufacture were associated with the highest number of reports of pet illnesses.

These inspections provided valuable information on these firms' jerky pet treat manufacturing operations, including ingredients, raw materials, as well as manufacturing equipment, heat treatment, packaging, quality control, sanitation, and product testing.

Although these inspections helped identify additional areas for investigation, we found no evidence indicating that these firms' jerky pet treats are associated with illnesses.

As a follow-up to those inspections we sent a delegation to China to express our concerns about the complaints we continue to receive. As a result, FDA and Chinese authorities agreed to expand investigation of jerky pet treats.

In addition to sharing our epidemiological findings, we have initiated a scientific collaboration with the Chinese and have taken other steps to identify the root cause of the illnesses. We also have hosted Chinese scientists at our veterinary research facility to further scientific cooperation.

Thank you again for this opportunity to describe our ongoing efforts to determine a definitive cause. If our investigation leads to identification of any particular jerky pet treat ingredient or contaminant that is associated with these illnesses, we intend to act quickly to notify the public and take steps as appropriate to ensure that these affected products are promptly removed from the market.

In the meantime, we encourage consumers to continue to check our Web site for updates and we continue to remind pet owners that jerky pet treats are not necessary for a pet's healthy diet, so eliminating them will not harm pets since commercially produced pet food contains all the ingredients that pets need.

Thank you very much again for having me today.

Chairman BROWN. Thank you, Ms. Forfa, very much.

My first set of questions will go to Dr. Engeljohn and then I'll turn it over to Congressman Smith. Then my second round will be with Ms. Forfa.

I think the American public is pretty confused about what labels mean and what exactly does "Made in the USA" mean; what does it mean when there is no country-of-origin label on a product? Let me get to that in a second.

It appears the assertion of processed chicken being labeled as from China hinges on the assumption that it has to be cooked in China, and cooked chicken coming over from China is not likely to be repackaged or further processed here in the United States.

So my question is this. This box of chicken mac-and-cheese says it's a product—this one says "Made in USA." This says "Made in the USA." The question is, is it possible that cooked chicken from China could end up—and this one doesn't say any country of origin, correct? This one has no country of origin.

So does this, if it says "Made in USA," mean always that the chicken was neither raw chicken nor—well, does it mean it's neither raw chicken nor packaged chicken nor processed chicken coming from China? If it says "Made in the USA," can you be confident that it wasn't here, then sent back to China, then here or does this always mean the supply chain is entirely made in the United States, it's entirely within the United States?

Mr. ENGELJOHN. Okay. So thank you for the question. On issues related to the meat or poultry products that you referenced, without looking at that box, I'm not real sure if that's a product that is regulated by my agency, from the perspective that if there's more than 2 percent poultry in that, as an example, then it would be regulated by my agency.

But on the issue of COOL, if it's a COOL-related policy, then that would be a policy that is administered by the Agricultural Marketing Service at USDA and not my agency. But the products that are contained within that statutory provision would be for covered commodities, which are generally just whole muscle cuts and ground meat. So with regard to processed meat products, they would not be covered by the COOL-related labeling to begin with.

In terms of voluntary labeling in terms of what that would mean, we don't have criteria that we use to set a basis for made in the United States.

Chairman BROWN. So what does that mean in terms of, if someone goes to the store and gets this chicken mac-and-cheese and it does say USDA on it, inspected, does this mean when I buy this at the local Heinen's in Cleveland that I will know that none of this came from China, that none of it was either processed in China or the raw chicken came from China? It sounds from your answer that I don't have, and you don't have, confidence that that's the case.

Mr. ENGELJOHN. Yes. I don't believe that that statement would fully cover the issue of product that may have come in, that may be a small portion that might be contained within that overall product.

Chairman BROWN. So what's the use of a product that says "Product of USA?" What's the use of that kind of label? What does that label tell us then?

Mr. ENGELJOHN. Yes. I think on a product such as that it would be the majority of ingredients in there would be from confirmed sources that were either slaughtered or processed within the United States. So it would be a majority, but I don't believe that you could identify that there would be no ingredients from another country, particularly if it was from another country that had an equivalent system because once it comes into the domestic system it becomes a U.S. product.

Chairman BROWN. Equivalent USDA/FDA regimen of consumer protection.

Mr. ENGELJOHN. Yes.

Chairman BROWN. Okay. Of food safety.

This box, which is chicken fettucine, has no country of origin label at all. What does that tell the consumer when she or he sees that?

Mr. ENGELJOHN. Again, in terms of—if it's a question about whether or not the——

Chairman BROWN. Excuse me. It presumably has well over 2 percent of the ingredients that are chicken.

Mr. ENGELJOHN. Right. So the COOL labeling, the country of origin labeling, would not be applicable to a product such as that. Again, for the meat products that would be covered, it would be whole-muscle cuts or ground products, they would not be processed products. So in this case, that would contain a mixture of processed products.

Chairman BROWN. I mean, the issue I'm trying to get at is not what technically falls in the jurisdiction of FDA or USDA or some other regulatory body. The question is what message does it send to American consumers about our food safety system? The question about the chicken mac-and-cheese, you talk about just the whole issue of how much or what percent of imported—perhaps imported chicken, processed chicken, might have.

We know from several years ago most of the drug heparin came from U.S. sources, but there were contaminants that came from China that caused people to die. So the percentages, while they may matter in statute and they may matter to regulators and to Members of the House or Senate perhaps, ultimately if they contaminate the food that someone ingests, that's fundamentally the issue.

So go back to this chicken fettucine, since there's no country of origin labeling. What would you suggest we do on something like this?

Mr. ENGELJOHN. So on products such as that—and again, the manufacturer of that product can choose whether or not they put in place a control program for the source ingredients that would be used in that product.

If they had the type of evidence to demonstrate that the source could be verified through a third party, as an example, a claim such as ''Made in the USA'' or some specific artifact such as that on the label then could be verified and that could be on the label.

Without there being a designation on that product, it could simply mean that the manufacturer did not source those materials and have verification for it, so it may or may not be completely from a product that is slaughtered, produced, and processed within the United States. It really does matter whether or not in this case the manufacturer has chosen to use ingredients and then seek a labeling claim for that.

At USDA, for the labeling of that product, it's a prior approval system for which we will look for the evidence that the manufac-

11

turer would submit to verify whether or not the ingredients are, in fact, verifiable.

Chairman BROWN. You spoke of equivalency of other food safety regulatory systems. I think most Americans would have confidence in a product processed in Canada because I think most Americans, or a number of Americans actually go to Canada to buy their prescription drugs, for instance, believing that the Canadian system of FDA, of regulatory safety for pharmaceuticals, is more or less equivalent to ours.

Understanding that, I wanted to ask about the audit that found China's poultry processing inspections system equivalent to ours in light of China's well-documented poor food safety record and corruption problems.

In terms of the audit that USDA conducted to make this determination, talk to us about how rigorous it was, how we can be assured that Chinese officials played it straight during that audit process.

Mr. ENGELJOHN. So, thank you on that question related to the audits. Actually, there were multiple audits that we conducted in China over the course of several years, originally back in 2004 when we started the process, and then again when we more recently reaffirmed that process.

As I had mentioned, we do rely upon the documentation the country submits to us to demonstrate that they have laws and regulations in place that are equivalent to the laws and regulations that we have at USDA for the products we regulate domestically. That's the first stage.

The second stage would be an actual on-site audit of their system where we would send auditors from the United States into the facilities that China would elect to demonstrate that their system is set up to be able to produce product in an equivalent manner as we do in the United States.

So our auditors from the United States would be there for an extended period of time, observing the slaughter of the animals and the processing of the animals if it's a slaughter equivalence audit, or in the case where it was the processed products then it was to look to ensure that the ingredients that were being used from a poultry perspective were from the United States or from an approved source, and then observe the actual fabrication and processing of that product along with the records.

With that, then they looked at the evidence that the country had for the microbiological tests and chemical tests that they would have conducted on that product. That serves as one basis in which we observed what is happening. We also assessed the laboratory procedures to ensure that their capability is such that they can discern the pathogens and chemical residues that we have a concern about.

Once we determine that the country has demonstrated that they're able to meet our expectations, which is the case for China on processed poultry, then they go through the rulemaking process and add them to our Federal regulations. We're at that final stage now on the process side where we've gone back since there was a period of time in which China was not actively seeking an approval for equivalence and they administered a new food safety law.

So we went back to reaffirm their process, that their new laws were still designed to meet the same equivalent outcome as what we have in the United States. So we observed, again. So that was another observation actually in the processing facilities where they were producing it.

Chairman BROWN. And I want to ask you about the equivalency of raw chicken in a minute. But are you confident then, do you have some certainty that you do those inspections, you go through the rulemaking process, you think they're doing their processing in an equivalent sort of way to the way we do it—are you confident that without USDA, without ongoing USDA inspections and U.S. inspectors at the right places in China, at these facilities in China, that they will continue to meet those standards?

Mr. ENGELJOHN. Yes. We're confident due to the process of our government relationship and our ongoing dialogue with the government officials that they're maintaining the inspection system that they in essence redesigned in order to meet the U.S. requirements.

I would add that on top of that the FSIS import requirements would be that we do have a point of entry reinspection requirement in which 100 percent of the shipments that come in from China are reinspected for a variety of issues related to proper labeling, proper certificates, condition of the products, the box count, and that the labeling is proper.

Then for new countries such as China that would be coming on board, we would have an intensified import reinspection where we would do more thorough inspections, including collecting samples for drug residues and for microbiological pathogens.

So the combination of having evidence that they have an inspection system which they redesigned, which they would continuously provide us information about how well that system is operating and the evidence that they have to demonstrate that, as well as the evidence that they have of training their employees and maintaining the competence of that system, the re-inspection serves as an important check on whether or not we find issues of concern that then we would go back and follow up with China.

So I think we have a system in place that has worked well for the 28 other countries that are actively exporting to this country and that process is ongoing. So once they had been deemed equivalent, we do have a process in place where we would reaffirm that over time.

Chairman BROWN. Let me switch to the raw chicken. As you noted, China was not granted equivalency status for its poultry slaughter system and cannot export, as a result, raw chicken to the United States, at least not yet. Is China requesting another audit? If so, when might that occur and how close was—if you'd give us your thoughts on how close China was to equivalency. Where did they fall short and how difficult will it be for them to correct that?

Mr. ENGELJOHN. So there are a couple of issues. I'll explain the process. The slaughter process, in and of itself, is one for which the domestic system for slaughter in China was different—considerably different—than it is for the domestic system in the United States.

So the process in which the establishments that China identified for the agency to audit required them to modify substantially the procedures that they would be using there in order to have equivalent procedures.

So I would say that the issues related to whether or not they're close to meeting our expectations for slaughter were, they were close to hitting the mark on that. We did respond with our concerns and they've responded back with their corrective measures for how they would address our concerns. They have not yet requested an audit for us to come back and look, although we expect that that would happen fairly soon.

Once we would go back, and if we were to determine that they are in fact capable of having an equivalent system, then that would start our rulemaking process where we would go through the process of putting out a Federal Register proposed rule to add China to our list of countries deemed eligible to ship slaughtered poultry to the United States.

Chairman BROWN. Let me interrupt for a second. Does any country that gets on that list, the eligibility list if you will, ever get off it as a result of a changed practice or not living up to the standards that it committed to and promised and practiced?

Mr. ENGELJOHN. What I would say is that there are countries that don't actively export, for reasons—either they've chosen because of the degree of difficulty or just the market access.

Chairman BROWN. If they continue to export, they continue to live up to that standard. At least that's been the evidence so far.

Mr. ENGELJOHN. That's right. So if they're on the list, but if they've been off from the list for a period of time then we would go back and reaffirm our understanding about their system. But removing a country, we have not, to my knowledge, removed it completely.

Chairman BROWN. And I know I interrupted your answer, but I want to get to one thing. I've taken a lot of time and I want Congressman Smith to certainly have his time.

If raw chicken from China is approved for export here, if you go through that process and you found equivalency, if it's exported from China and imported into the United States it's processed in the United States, what will the label say? Will it say country of origin China or will it say ''Made in the USA,'' or let's say neither of those things?

Mr. ENGELJOHN. Okay. So I would like to just add that, in addition to the FSIS requirements for equivalency there is an animal health issue that has to be dealt with for our Animal and Plant Health Inspection Service, which at the moment is one of the reasons why poultry cannot be—even if FSIS were to move forward with this portion of the rulemaking, there's still the issue of dealing with the animal disease, and in this case avian influenza, that has to be addressed. It's the reason why cooked poultry only can come in from China.

But having said that and if those issues were resolved, then if product coming in from China is a raw poultry product it would fit the expectations for a whole muscle cut that COOL regulations would define right now that would require labeling. But the fact that the product is produced in a certified establishment in China would also identify the establishment name and number on the product, so it would be identified as a product of China.

Once that product then came into the United States and is put into the domestic system, if it didn't go directly to retail and was used as an ingredient in product that is being manufactured domestically, then it becomes domestic product and it would not bear the labeling of "Made in China."

Chairman BROWN. But I assume that you're comfortable with that because you are comfortable with the fact that the raw chicken at this point, once it's certified, is in fact equivalent and safe.

Mr. ENGELJOHN. We move forward with our determination that there's an equivalent system and it's based upon a totality of information that we believe would, in fact, demonstrate that the country is capable of ongoing inspecting of that product and producing it safely to meet the expectations of the United States, then with our reinspection requirements, providing an added measure of looking for issues of concern.

So if we had reason to believe that there were chemicals or drugs used on products that perhaps are not used in the United States, if we were aware of that, then we would likely build that into our re-inspection procedures at the port of entry and look for it there, as well as querying the government to provide us evidence as to whether or not there are drugs or other compounds used that likely are not deemed to be safe in the United States.

Chairman BROWN. Let me go a slightly different place then turn it over to Congressman Smith. You talked about facilities where there will be inspections for either the raw or processed chicken in China. I ran a hearing about five years ago on the sort of supply chain for pharmaceuticals in China and that the ingredients were made or the ingredients would often come from sort of mom-and-pop operations all over villages, all over this country of 1.3 billion people in an area more or less the size of the 48 contiguous states in the United States.

What is the reach of this? Roughly how many facilities do you or would you inspect, would you need to inspect in China for either the processed or the raw chicken to make our food supply safe?

Mr. ENGELJOHN. With regard to the FSIS equivalence process, we would be focused solely on the slaughter or processing facilities. So the other facilities producing other ingredients that might be used would not be part of the review of FSIS.

However, what we would ask and have evidence from the Chinese Government for would be evidence that the ingredients to be used in the meat or poultry products, that we would find to be in line with export to the United States and would need to come from sources that are approved for food use and have in place, in essence, evidence to suggest and demonstrate that that ingredient is in fact safe for that use.

Chairman BROWN. So how many of those facilities are there, the slaughtering facilities?

Mr. ENGELJOHN. Well, presently there are four establishments that China has identified that, if and when they begin exporting to the United States——

Chairman BROWN. All of it would come through those four?

Mr. ENGELJOHN. They would only come from those four facilities at this time. Should China choose to put in place an inspection system in additional facilities, then they would identify what they have done to ensure that those facilities meet our expectations. FSIS then would have the opportunity, should we choose to go and conduct audits in those facilities, we certainly could do so, but we rely upon the government to tell us which facilities. But right now, only four.

Chairman BROWN. So those inspections at the place where you found equivalence with the food, but the processing, chicken processing, how many of those facilities are there? It's not those four. It would be different facilities, right?

Mr. ENGELJOHN. Yes. China has a large number of establishments but they have only put forward four for which they have——

Chairman BROWN. For the raw chicken.

Mr. ENGELJOHN. For the processing and——

Chairman BROWN. Oh. Processing and——

Mr. ENGELJOHN. Yes.

Chairman BROWN. The processing and raw poultry.

Mr. ENGELJOHN. For right now it's just processed poultry, is what we're focused upon because that's where they have, in fact, identified that they have put in place inspection systems demonstrated to meet our expectations.

Chairman BROWN. Okay. Okay. Thank you. Sorry I took so long.

Representative SMITH. Thank you very much, Mr. Chairman.

Thank you for your testimony and for your insights. Let me just ask you, Dr. Engeljohn, how many of the other 28 countries are democracies, how many are dictatorships?

Mr. ENGELJOHN. I'm sorry, I don't know the answer to that question.

Representative SMITH. Could you name some of the countries?

Mr. ENGELJOHN. Certainly. So for the—I would just—are you interested in the countries that have approved sources for poultry, as an example, and others?

Representative SMITH. Primarily. What we're looking at is, and you've said it several times today, that we're relying on government. We rely on the government's documentation on site. When we're dealing with a democracy, obviously there's transparency, there's whistleblowers.

I mean, what happens if a Chinese employee or someone anywhere in the chain of command over there blows the whistle? Does he or she go to jail or do they get a promotion? Whistleblowers are sometimes not well heeded anywhere else either, but they play an absolutely important role, and bloggers and journalists who also do whistleblowing. The people inside the factory or the slaughterhouse, what happens? Have there been any instances where there has been a whistleblower who is Chinese?

Mr. ENGELJOHN. If I may, I'll answer the question about the countries eligible to ship poultry to the United States with equivalent systems that are actively doing so; so Canada, Chile, France, Great Britain, Hong Kong, and Israel. Then Australia and New Zealand are approved to do so, but only for ratites, so it's a very specific type of poultry. Then Mexico and China are the two presently that are listed in our regulations for processed poultry.

Representative SMITH. So from that list it would appear that the only dictatorship is China. As Chairman Brown and I and our Commission has documented, especially through the annual human rights report that comes out, the word of the Chinese Government is usually not trustworthy. I have found very few instances in my 44 years as a Member of Congress where I took on face value just about anything the government said, whether it be about political prisoners or any other situation.

There's always, every time, laced in there a whole drill of misinformation and lies and deceit. If that's the modus operandi for how they deal with all things related to democracy and human rights, it's not a stretch to say if we rely on them for documentation, that's an Achilles heel that is huge. Would you agree?

Mr. ENGELJOHN. Well, it does present a huge dilemma. I would say though that our on-site audits and our ongoing re-inspection at ports of entry into the United States provide us additional levels of safety concerns that we can have oversight over, and then we do respond to the press.

We respond to issues that we hear about of concern that might be ongoing anyplace around the world and in terms of whether or not we need to step up a particular re-inspection activity or we need to go back and conduct audits to investigate a particular issue.

Representative SMITH. When you do an audit, what kind of access do we have to the plant or the processing facility? Is it immediate or do we have to give advance notice? Is it unfettered? Do the people who go speak fluent Chinese? Are they able to talk to workers without that worker being retaliated against, or do we look at paper?

Mr. ENGELJOHN. Okay. So we have reciprocal response between other countries coming to the United States and auditing our system versus us going to other countries, so we do have advanced notification when we are going there.

Representative SMITH. How far in advance?

Mr. ENGELJOHN. Well, it's typically far enough in advance to be able to arrange travel, get visas, and those types of things approved. So we do have to go through that process for countries where visas are required.

Representative SMITH. How long does it usually take?

Mr. ENGELJOHN. I would say usually 60 days in advance.

Representative SMITH. Sixty days?

Mr. ENGELJOHN. In order to plan that type of audit or visit that we would need to make.

Representative SMITH. So if there is some compelling information, we don't have people either in the Embassy who will be mobilized immediately to go check this out or someone who could get there, get the visa for whatever reason, and just get there for an on-site inspection where you don't get a Potemkin Village?

Mr. ENGELJOHN. So what I would say is we're fortunate in that, as an example, in China where we do have a presence, USDA does have a staff that is present there, interacting with the government, and does have access throughout the country.

When we do go into a country we have translators with us and we do have access to the facilities as we would here. A facility that is receiving the grant of inspection is required to give us full access to all the records and presence whenever we need to be there.

Representative SMITH. Could the records be falsified that they get to look at?

Mr. ENGELJOHN. They could be. They could be here as well. So our process is——

Representative SMITH. Well, here they can be prosecuted. Here they can be prosecuted in a court where the judicial system, despite its flaws, is above board.

Mr. ENGELJOHN. Yes. And our auditors, as an example, when they do go and look at in-country as well as the documentation that we require the country to submit annually, are looking very thoroughly at the records to see whether or not there is the potential for evidence of falsification. Again, we do have some cross-checks in that we can test for microorganisms and pathogens in order to have additional confidence to what we would find.

Representative SMITH. How many inspectors and personnel are dedicated to these Chinese products? How many people are we talking about?

Mr. ENGELJOHN. In China? I'm sorry.

Representative SMITH. No, for the whole—your operation. How often do they actually get deployed to China to do inspections?

Mr. ENGELJOHN. Okay. Generally speaking, again, we have a presence. The U.S. Department of Agriculture [USDA] has a presence there in terms of permanent staff that is located in-country, and APHIS, our sister agency at USDA, as well has a staff there. When FSIS sends a team in-country it's usually a team perhaps of 6 to 10 individuals, all with differing expertise, whether it be microbiology, veterinary medicine, epidemiology, policy, those types of things.

So it's a team of diverse subject matter experts that are there for an extended period of time. They are with translators who will be translating for the U.S. Government, not Chinese employees but U.S. Government-sanctioned interpreters.

Representative SMITH. Has there ever been a situation where you didn't have enough people in the pool where the 6 to 10 were deployed and others had to wait in order to do an inspection or did you get that few of requests.

Mr. ENGELJOHN. An agency such as ours with roughly 7,800 employees and very dedicated staff of professionals, we have the resources that we need to put it together.

Representative SMITH. So the pull-down in personnel comes from that larger group?

Mr. ENGELJOHN. That's right.

Representative SMITH. Do they have specialized training in dealing with audits that could be easily falsified?

Mr. ENGELJOHN. Yes. Our auditors are specifically trained as auditors. Then the subject matter experts that join them are there with their subject matter expertise.

Representative SMITH. Well, I raise this in part because even when we were talking about groups like Apple Computer, auditors were paid to falsify and then to give a clean bill of health to the corporation that everything's just fine, gulag labor, slave labor type conditions are not occurring when certain products are being made. I mean, this is the land of disinformation.

Unless somebody is very adept at looking and asking—and again, maybe you did answer it even here, but do you know of any instance where a whistleblower came forward who happened to be a Chinese man or woman, who came forward and said this product is adulterated, this, if you will, Omega-3 fish oil is nothing but adulterated, this honey has been filled with something other than honey even though it says Grade A Clover, or whatever. Do you have any instance where whistleblowers came forward?

Mr. ENGELJOHN. Not for issues relating to FSIS products, no.

Representative SMITH. If you hear of something, if you could let us know because it would be nice to know what happens to that person. Do they get prosecuted, taken out in the back and put into a van? Because again, this is a dictatorship. I can't stress that enough, in terms of my sense.

I mean, I am working on the whole false solution that when we're talking about gulag labor we started with Bush One, carried into Clinton, carried right up to this day where Customs would be able to check out whether or not something was being made with gulag labor, which we know it does.

I was actually in Beijing Prison Number 1 right after Tiananmen Square in 1991, so a couple of years later, and they were making Jellies socks and shoes for export. And only because we literally took with us the Jellies socks were we able to get an import ban on those gulag-made goods.

I'm sure the records were great. That stuff was showing up all over in the United States. Jellies shoes were big for little girls at the time. But only because we had—we have Customs people who are supposed to be doing this and they're like the Maytag repairman.

So if it happens in this realm, I don't know why it wouldn't happen in the food or the pet realm where there are huge profits to be made if you can cut corners, and corruption obviously moves higher in dictatorships than it does when you have checks and balances. So, just some thoughts on that.

Let me ask you, if I could, Mr. Assistant Administrator, can any chicken processed in China end up in school lunches or other Federal meal programs? And would you clarify why the USDA believes that processed poultry from China would not be repackaged or further processed in the United States? And if any of it was, would it require labels saying "Processed in China?"

Mr. ENGELJOHN. Okay. I would answer that. The questions on the school lunch program are handled by our Agricultural Marketing Service and our Food and Nutrition Service at USDA, so for more specific information we certainly can get information back to you on that.

Representative SMITH. Thank you, for the record.

Mr. ENGELJOHN. But with regard to product requirements, I can tell you that for the National School Lunch Program, the Agricultural Marketing Service does buy only American product. So for that purpose, products sourced from China would not meet those expectations.

The question though about, why do we believe product would likely not be repackaged, the issue being that product would be coming from the United States, Chile, or Canada, one of the approved countries to slaughter the poultry, go to China, be processed, come back here in consumer-ready packaging. So it would be coming back as cooked consumer-ready product.

The likelihood of that being then taken and rounded up and added to other products domestically, we think, is a low likelihood. It could happen, but we think that that likely would not be the case. As such, that product would be available in the marketplace for the consumer to see that it is made in China.

Representative SMITH. I have one last question.

Several years ago I chaired a landmark hearing on censorship on the Internet. We had Google, Microsoft, Cisco, and Yahoo! all testify. I swore them all in. They all said how they were just following the Chinese law, leaving it all up to the Chinese to tell us what they could censor and what they should not, and wouldn't tell any of us at the hearing what they were doing, words like the Dalai Lama and all the other things that were excised when you did a Google search, or any other search, there.

The Internet is so heavily censored. How does a Chinese person—again, going back to this idea that, can we trust anything this government says? I wish we could. I really wish they were trading partners rather than adversaries, as they are around the world, particularly in Africa.

So if you could, the Internet. If somebody went and blogged tomorrow that poultry processing plant A, B, or C is a huge problem and this is why, what would happen?

Mr. ENGELJOHN. I did say—again, we're pre—given final approval in terms of moving forward with the equivalence process in China. But I think any information like that is what we do assess. We hear reports of issues of concern.

If we knew that one of the facilities that was deemed to be certified by China was one of those plants that a consumer in China were to identify, it would cause us to look into and be concerned about that and likely be part of questions that we would ask the Chinese Government and then be part of an audit process if and when we do go back to China, which we would expect to do.

Representative SMITH. Thank you.

Chairman BROWN. Thank you. There is a vote expected at 4:45 on our side, so I will ask Ms. Forfa questions for maybe 10 minutes and then if you complete your discussion with her you can go to the next panel. But we'll work that out.

Ms. Forfa, give us an update on PEDv and where you see it going, when you think you will know enough to get to the bottom of this? If you would just give us a progress update.

Ms. FORFA. Sure. So we are continuing our investigation and we are working with our counterparts in the Canadian foods inspection authority as well as our counterparts at USDA, APHIS, on the investigation. I don't have any definitive idea when that investigation will be closed, but we do continue to pursue that actively.

Chairman BROWN. Okay. Do you feel like, as you've pursued this and figured this out and made some progress in doing that, is there a system in place to catch this in the future before something like this can happen?

Ms. FORFA. Without knowing and certainly identifying a definitive cause of the outbreak—this particular virus was found in the

1970s in Britain, so it's been around for a while. My experts tell me that it is fairly widespread globally and so the investigation will be complex. So we just need to do a real scientific study and do some trace-back and figure out if we can identify the source.

Chairman BROWN. Let me talk about visas and FDA. My understanding is the FDA is increasing inspectors in China but that China is holding up visas for those inspectors. Vice President Biden brought this issue up with the Chinese in December. What kind of progress have we seen?

Ms. FORFA. We have made progress. Things have been moving forward since Vice President Biden was there in December of last year. We are moving to get those visas in place and increase our presence in our China office, which we have found very helpful.

Chairman BROWN. Is the progress sufficient? Are you satisfied that you have gotten enough visas or are you just saying it's better than it was?

Ms. FORFA. We are moving forward.

Chairman BROWN. Sounds like a fairly low bar that satisfies you.

Ms. FORFA. I think we are encouraged by the progress that's being made.

Chairman BROWN. So it is a low bar. Okay.

Talk about labor. This is a—got to love this product. It's called ''Happy Hips,'' and it's got glucosamine and chondroitin for your dog's joints, apparently. It says natural with added glucosamine, chondroitin, and vitamin E. No grain, corn, wheat, soy, or fillers. Treatment for adult dogs. American flag on it, ''Made in the USA.''

Now, given our current labeling laws, they can put this on here. My question is, could this also include a relatively small amount that includes vitamins or other additives from China and still put the label—slap the American flag on there and say ''Made in the USA? ''

Ms. FORFA. We don't have primary labeling authority for country of origin, that's Customs and Border Protection that actually has the primary requirement for labeling. We require that manufacturers put on their labeling the ingredients and then the name and their place of business.

Chairman BROWN. So there is some traceability there.

Ms. FORFA. Yes.

Chairman BROWN. And if someone from that agency were sitting in that third chair, would—let me back up. Do you know enough about this sort of larger system than your, not to imply narrow, but narrower authority here? Do you know enough to be able to describe or to be able to say definitively that all these ingredients come from the United States?

Ms. FORFA. I would be happy to get back to you on that.

Chairman BROWN. So I mean, I know in response to some of the issues with pet treats, with dogs getting sick, with dogs dying in some cases, with not yet always proving what happened but the fear that some pet owners have, that I know of pet owners who now buy things only with an American flag or only ''Made in the USA.'' But you're not willing to definitely say that every ingredient in here in fact comes from the United States?

Ms. FORFA. I will be happy to get back to you. I will be happy to look into that and get back to you on that.

Chairman BROWN. Okay. Okay.

Ms. FORFA. I'm always reluctant to give definitives.

Chairman BROWN. No, I understand that. Last question, if I could. I understand that FDA works with the Centers for Disease Control and Prevention [CDC] on the pet treats issue. Talk to me about the coordination and information sharing. Are you satisfied with that?

Ms. FORFA. Certainly. I'd be happy to, actually. This is a rather unique situation because normally we don't have a CDC-type infrastructure for pet-related illnesses. We did reach out to our colleagues at CDC and ask them for help in doing a case control study and helping us with some of our epidemiologic work.

They are currently working on a case-control study for us where they are calling pet owners whose dogs had reported cases of illnesses and comparing those to those controls, controls they picked in similar geographic areas where no pet illnesses were reported.

This was done just recently and we don't have the results back yet, but we are very grateful to our colleagues at CDC for their willingness to—they came up and met with us—and for undertaking this case-control study with us.

Chairman BROWN. Okay. Last question. I am, in a couple of minutes, going to turn it over to Congressman Smith.

There's a common perception that pet food treats are not fairly regulated here, and less so in China. I think from Congressman Smith's opening statement about Upton Sinclair and ''The Jungle,'' I think that people in this country, except those who think government has no role in anything, are pretty satisfied that we do a pretty good job in this country with our food supply, with our pharmaceutical supply, and with water and generally issues around what we eat and what we breathe, and what we drink.

How much is—if in fact this is—did come entirely from the United States, if all the ingredients in Happy Hips came from the United States, should people be confident that we inspect well enough our own facilities and make sure that these products are in fact safe for pets?

Ms. FORFA. We consider pet food—while it has some differences, we consider it very similar to food. It needs to have ingredients, it needs to be properly labeled, so we work very hard to ensure that the American pet food supply is safe.

Chairman BROWN. But you still couldn't answer the question, that this pet food, if this is entirely from the United States, that every ingredient is in fact from the United States. You can't assure us of that until you get back to us, though?

Ms. FORFA. Correct.

Chairman BROWN. Okay. All right. Thank you.

Ms. FORFA. Thank you.

Chairman BROWN. Mr. Smith?

Representative SMITH [presiding]. Thank you very much, Mr. Chairman.

Just briefly—I do have a lot of questions but I'll submit some more for the record—just on the visa delay, how many visas have been delayed or denied?

Ms. FORFA. That, I will have to get back to you on.

[The information appears in the appendix.]

Representative SMITH. Because again, I would share the concern with my good friend and colleague Chairman Brown. Not only is that a low bar, it should be a red flag. I mean, what are they hiding? Why are they unwilling? I mean, I can't get a visa to go there, at least not recently, because of human rights work. But for people to be coming in to do your vital mission to protect American end consumers as well as those who have pets, that raises a lot of questions.

Let me ask you, Doctor, if I could. Shaun Kennedy is the director of the Food System Institute at the University of Minnesota. In his testimony he talks about, if the problem is low-level contamination and cumulative doses are the reasons for the illness, it could unfortunately take much more time to figure out. Whether for human or for animal food, there are more of those for chronic toxicity than with acute toxicity.

This becomes even more important for both infants and pets, who tend to have the same limited sets of foods over time so that a low level of contamination in the treats, sometimes not considered an acute health risk, could lead to chronic illness with a steady dose of treats over time.

How do you screen that out, long-term cumulative dosing of toxic substances that get into either an infant or a person's system, or a pet? Who's looking for that?

Ms. FORFA. Many of the illnesses that we've seen are acute.

Representative SMITH. Right.

Ms. FORFA. And so we have an incredible team working on this. We have epidemiologists, toxicologists, veterinary researchers, including the woman who was able to crack the melamine code in 2007. So we have put all of our experts on this and we've screened for a number of things that would cause the types of illnesses we've seen, including salmonella, metals, markers of irradiation, pesticides, antibiotics, anti-virals, molds, rodenticides, nephrotoxins, because the illnesses of most concern to us are the kidney issues.

So we're particularly focused on nephrotoxins and any other chemical or poisonous compounds that we can think of that would cause these types of illness patterns that we've seen. We have also reached out through a wide network that we've developed to private universities and laboratories and our state counterparts to make sure that we have all of the laboratory expertise that we possibly can to screen for everything that they can think of. So I'm confident that while we haven't found a definitive cause, we are covering the waterfront to the best of our ability.

Representative SMITH. And can you assure us that there's a robust surveillance on long-term toxicity?

Ms. FORFA. While on the animal side we don't have the same sort of surveillance system that we do on the human side through the Centers for Disease Control and state public health partners, since melamine we have instituted a number of reporting portals, including a pet food reporting portal and a number of other reporting tools for veterinarians to be able to get the information to us so that we can do our own surveillance work.

Representative SMITH. Now, is China shipping processed chicken to other nations?

Mr. ENGELJOHN. Yes.

Representative SMITH. Are they concerned about the inadequate slaughter and the process that's involved?

Mr. ENGELJOHN. I'm not aware of the requirements other countries have with regard to their equivalency type process for countries.

Representative SMITH. Okay. If I were shipping to any countries like in Europe where they might have a heightened concern about food safety?

Mr. ENGELJOHN. I don't have specifics on that, but we certainly can follow up and let you know what we can find out.

Representative SMITH. Okay.

Representative SMITH. Just one thought. I chaired a hearing on Nigeria not so long ago on counterfeit products, pharmaceuticals and the like. Many of our witnesses came in and held up one that was made as a counterfeit to an American product that said "Made in America" but was made in China, and one product after another—I don't know if it applied to chicken, processed chicken, but again the idea that a country that so mistreats its own people with its human rights abuse, and lacks transparency to the nth degree—can it be counted on to come clean on ensuring that products are what they say they are and have been processed the way they ought to have been processed? It's a very threshold question but one that I struggle with.

I am out of my questions, but I think we need to move on. So I guess I'll just thank you both. Look forward to hearing back from you on some of the questions that you need some further elaboration on, but thank you again for your work. Appreciate it.

Ms. FORFA. Thank you.

Representative SMITH. I'd like to now welcome to the witness table our second panel.

[Pause.]

Representative SMITH. I'd like to introduce our very distinguished panel, panel two, beginning with Shaun Kennedy, who is Director of the Food System Institute and an adjunct associate professor in the Department of Veterinary Population Medicine at the University of Minnesota's College of Veterinary Medicine.

Previously, Professor Kennedy was an associate professor with Food Systems at the University of Minnesota, where he also served as director of the National Center for Food Production and Defense.

Then we'll hear from Patty Lovera, who is the assistant director of Food & Water Watch and runs the organization's food policy team. Before joining Food & Water Watch, Ms. Lovera was the deputy director of the energy and environment program at Public Citizen, and a researcher at the Center for Health, Environment and Justice.

Then we'll hear from Christopher D'Urso, who is a consumer advocate and graduating senior at the Law & Public Service Learning Center at Colts Neck High School in Colts Neck, and as I indicated earlier he has actually provided extraordinarily useful information to my staff and me. He really is an advocate for revamping country of origin labeling laws, and he's been doing that since 2012.

So Professor Kennedy, if you could begin.

STATEMENT OF SHAUN KENNEDY, DIRECTOR, FOOD SYSTEM INSTITUTE, LLC; ADJUNCT ASSOCIATE PROFESSOR, DEPARTMENT OF VETERINARY POPULATION MEDICINE, COLLEGE OF VETERINARY MEDICINE, UNIVERSITY OF MINNESOTA

Mr. KENNEDY. Thank you, Cochairman Smith, for the introduction. And thank you, Chairman Brown and the members of the Commission, for the opportunity to speak to you today about the current concerns of the safety of the food and feed system and how we might be able to make it safer.

As a proud owner of Storm, an Aussiedoodle, the pet treat problem is personally troubling. That the treats are chicken jerky raises concerns over USDA's designation of China as an equal-to country for processed poultry.

The potential of the ongoing PEDv outbreak in swine may be attributable to feed is another example of uncertain food risk. Among many possible solutions to these food system concerns are demands for increased inspection and country-of-origin labeling [COOL]. Before addressing either I'd like to provide a bit of context around our food and agriculture system.

It is often hard to conceptualize how global our food system really is. In the first four months of this year, we imported food from more than 179 new countries, totaling $48 billion and 26 million tons. Focusing on consumer-oriented foods, we imported $23.5 billion and 11 million tons. That's 75 pounds per person, or over half a pound a day. We are always eating food that comes from around the world, from over 88,000 domestic and 116,000 foreign facilities.

Figuring out the origin of each ingredient in a meal is a significant challenge, but where it could come from is easier. If your lunch is a cheeseburger, French fries, and milk, the last two are fairly easy. We're a big producer of milk and French fries, importing either from only a few countries, mostly Canada, although the vitamins in milk are mostly imported. The cheeseburger is more of a challenge, as it components last year contained 75 or more individual ingredients that are imported from over 55 countries, providing billions of possible combinations of country of origin.

Sources may change several times a year. Ingredients also may be commingled in entirely different ways at different times. Clearly, accurate and informative COOL is thus a challenge.

The only reasonable option might be to provide the information on something like a QR [quick response] code for access to details that cannot be reasonably provided on the label. Whatever the solution, there is an additional expense. The scale and complexity also contributes to the challenge of ensuring our food is safe and how we can figure out when things go wrong.

As you heard with the pet treats, no causative agent has been identified. Without knowing what is causing the illness, and thus no means of screening products, firms and authorities have limited options. Purina has moved to a dedicated, direct supply chain in China for its pet treat production to better ensure their safety, but until the cause of illness is known, even that may not be enough.

When the cause of illness is known, inspection and testing have limited utility in protecting public health. Inspections have many benefits, including ensuring that the food safety system design meets all the requirements. They do not, however, provide assurance of no food-borne illness risk. That would require 100 percent inspection of every step and that is simply not achievable.

Under the Food Safety Modernization Act [FSMA], facilities have to be inspected every three to five years and it is already well beyond the resources currently available to FDA. Even annual inspections would not ensure the safety of any specific food.

Similarly, for product testing to provide 100 percent assurance of safety would require testing all servings of the product, leaving very little to actually eat. Product testing is still an important part of an effective food safety plan and it provides monitoring of the food safety system. You first have to know what to test for and how you're going to test and, for pet treats, we don't yet know.

With this ongoing concern, granting "equal to" status for processed poultry from China may seem odd, but that does not mean the consumer is going to be exposed to dramatically new food-borne illness threats from processed poultry in China. Since 2010, there have been five multi-state food-borne illness outbreaks associated with U.S. poultry, so there is already some level of food-borne illness risk.

One of the absolute best poultry plants I have ever conducted an audit on was actually in China. That facility's food safety system was driven primarily by its company standards and customer expectations, and that is very common. So while there is some baseline risk of illness due to consumption of food from any country, the real answer lies in the specific food systems, the visibility firms have of them, and how they are managed.

While not yet confirmed, feed has been strongly implicated in PEDv. Testing, however, has not confirmed feed is a source of any outbreak or that there is broad contamination of feed. With PEDv it's not just the animal that eats the feed that gets sick, but also those it infects, so given PEDv's low infected dose, low sporadic contamination of the feed or its packaging could spread the virus broadly. So even a robust testing strategy capable of detecting low levels of virus in every batch could not match the effective sampling strategy of feeding tens of thousands of pigs where only a few of the servings would have to be contaminated.

To summarize, until the cause of the pet illness is understood, import inspections and recalls provide no assurance of safety. Even when the source is understood, it will still be more effective for firms to manage their supply chains to mitigate continued exposure.

As is the case for domestic sourcing with appropriate due diligence, importers will have the ability to maintain the safety of the proposed processing of poultry products from China. If the feed system is proven to be the means by which PEDv is spread, sampling and testing of feed and feed ingredients will be a necessary but insufficient means of protecting the swine industry.

COOL is not as simple as it sounds, but technology-based solutions make it more realistic. In each case, supply chain visibility is a key part. While the overall food and agriculture system does a remarkable job of safely feeding us, we should do better. For effective partnerships across stakeholders, the encouraging thing is, we can.

I thank you for your time.

Representative SMITH. Professor Kennedy, thank you very much for your testimony and for your longer statement, which went into even greater detail. I appreciate it.

Without objections, all of your longer statements will be made a part of the record, but please feel free to use as much of it as you would like.

[The prepared statement of Professor Kennedy appears in the appendix.]

Representative SMITH. Ms. Lovera?

STATEMENT OF PATTY LOVERA, ASSISTANT DIRECTOR, FOOD & WATER WATCH

Ms. LOVERA. Good afternoon. My name is Patty Lovera and I am the assistant director of Food & Water Watch, a nonprofit consumer advocacy organization. Thank you so much for the opportunity to present testimony on this important topic.

The United States is increasingly reliant on imported food and China is a growing supplier of the food imports that are entering the U.S. China is the world's leading producer of many foods that Americans eat and it's also a leading producer of many of the inputs used to make processed food, and I discuss that in a lot more detail in my longer written testimony.

But the poorly controlled expansion of China's economy is often fueled by excess pollution, treacherous working conditions, and dangerous foods and products that pose significant risk to consumers in China and worldwide.

U.S. oversight of China's food processors has not remotely kept pace with the growth in these imports. Just as one example, the inspection rate that the Food and Drug Administration can maintain for imported food products means that less than 2 percent receive inspection.

The list of products imported from China may soon grow, as the USDA is considering allowing processed poultry products to enter the United States from China. This is a process that has been going on for several years. We've had rounds of audits, as you just heard, many of which revealed significant problems in the food safety system in these plants. There's been a World Trade Organization complaint that's gone several rounds on this, and we've even seen congressional intervention to block these imports, we think for good reason.

As we heard earlier in the earlier panel, the USDA has said that the inspection system of the Chinese Government for processed products is equivalent to ours, and so once the Chinese Government certifies those plants that they say are eligible, we could see these shipments begin.

The chickens were supposed to come from approved sources, which would not be China, but places like the United States or Canada. But we are extremely concerned that without having USDA inspectors in these Chinese processing plants, it would be virtually impossible to verify that these products are made from birds from these approved sources.

You heard a little bit in the first panel as well about relying on re-entry inspection and what happens at the border. While poultry products are not yet coming in from China, we are getting a lot of examples of the attacks that happen on that re-inspection system, whether it's products from Canada or other countries, and relying on that as a backstop makes us very, very nervous, as opposed to dealing with the real questions of whether the inspection system in the origin country is strong enough to start with.

There are also concerns about the potential for processed poultry products from China to end up in school cafeterias. There are a few inter-related policies happening. While the National School Lunch program run by the USDA is supposed to source domestic product, much of the food that schools buy doesn't come through that program. They can go to the open market, to private vendors.

They are supposed to look for U.S.-origin products to the maximum extent possible, but if the products don't have a label or schools have cost pressures that make them choose something else, we're afraid that that's a route for this Chinese origin product to end up in school cafeterias.

There's also a definition problem about what a U.S. product is in the school lunch venue. If over 51 percent of the content in a very processed product, like a burrito, is from the United States, the other 49 percent doesn't have to be. So that's another avenue that we're worried about.

To move on to the pet food issue, we think this is becoming a classic example of the transparency issues that we have heard about. In August 2012, the FDA published inspection reports that revealed that Chinese pet treat factories refused to allow U.S. inspectors to collect samples for independent analysis, and shortly after that we heard about the New York State Department of Agriculture and Markets doing their own testing and finding violative antibiotics that were not supposed to be used in poultry.

So we have a lot more that we need to do on the safety front, but I do want to spend my last minute talking about what consumers see in the marketplace because I'm a consumer advocate.

Representative SMITH. Don't hurry.

Ms. LOVERA. Okay. We have a lot to do on safety. I put a lot of recommendations in my longer testimony about that. But at a minimum, in the day-to-day while we're dealing with these safety problems, consumers need accurate information so they can make good decisions for themselves, and they're not getting it. If we're talking about either pet treats or processed poultry products, there's a lot of loopholes combining to make it very hard for consumers to navigate this.

So, despite a very long battle that we're still waging in the courts and at the World Trade Organization, we do have country of origin labeling for agricultural commodities like meats and poultry and fruits and vegetables, but that breaks down when we start to get into these processed foods because they're exempt from labeling requirements.

The way that USDA has defined that exemption leaves a lot of foods uncovered, and we're very concerned that a lot of these processed poultry products could be uncovered. When we move on to pet treats, there is even less labeling for consumers to access.

So we've heard a little bit about the varying ways it combines, but just because the definition of where a product's origin is depends on where it was substantially transformed, this could mean a low-value commodity being transformed into a more valuable processed product. That can determine the origin, which could be confusing for consumers if that commodity they're concerned about is chicken that comes from a place like China.

So we have a long list of recommendations in my longer testimony, but I will pull out just a couple. We think that it's time to start over evaluating this process of whether China is equivalent to USDA in inspection. There's a lot more that FDA needs to be doing to deal with increasing food imports from China, and we're very concerned about one mandate that is happening, that they rely on third party certifications as opposed to FDA inspection.

Then there is a lot that needs to be done for consumers to get better information. We need to fix these loopholes in country of origin labeling under the Farm Bill about what "processed" means, and then we also need to bring in these other agencies, Customs and also the Federal Trade Commission, to figure out what coverage we have for these other processed foods.

One example that we could look at is imported juice. There are special rules for juice because we're bringing in concentrate, blending it together here, and consumers do get more information about that because a policy was written to give people that origin information. So, we think that that is an avenue to explore.

So, thank you.

[The prepared statement of Ms. Lovera appears in the appendix.]

Representative SMITH. Thank you very much for your testimony and for your extensive recommendations at the end of it. I just read through it. It's excellent.

Mr. D'Urso?

STATEMENT OF CHRISTOPHER J. D'URSO, GRADUATING SENIOR, LAW & PUBLIC SERVICE LEARNING CENTER, COLTS NECK HIGH SCHOOL, COLTS NECK, NJ

Mr. D'URSO. Chairman Brown, Cochairman Smith, and distinguished members of the Commission, I am extremely grateful and honored to participate in this hearing.

My efforts to promote revamping country of origin labeling [COOL] laws resulted from an unfortunate experience before Christmas 2011. After eating my family's pignoli cookies, I suffered from pine mouth, a bitter metallic taste that lasted for several days. I soon discovered this was caused by a cheaper, inedible species of pine nuts which are commonly substituted by unscrupulous Chinese companies. Upon examining the bag of pine nuts, I was shocked to learn it did not have COOL, and consequently investigated why this was the case.

Under the Tariff Act of 1930 and the Farm Bills of 2002 and 2008, food products, dietary supplements, and pharmaceuticals do not need to have COOL if they are made in the United States or imported and processed in the United States. Unfortunately, these laws do not explicitly define processing, which has been too broadly interpreted to potentially include roasting peanuts and mixing peas with carrots. Equally disturbing, chicken that is slaughtered in the United States can be exported to China for processing and subsequently re-exported to the United States as a nugget or soup, potentially without COOL. The Congressional Research Service estimates that only 11 percent of pork, 30 percent of beef, 39 percent of chicken, and 40 percent of fruits and vegetables may be required to have COOL. The remainders are either produced in the United States or imported and processed in the United States. However, consumers will not know the reason. Regardless of the circumstances, all foods, dietary supplements, and pharmaceuticals should have COOL in order to protect consumer rights, public health, and American businesses.

Primarily, consumers have the fundamental right to know information about products in order to make informed purchasing decisions. Increasing imports from countries such as China may pose significant safety concerns. Alarmingly, the FDA admits it ''does not—nor will it—have the resources to adequately keep pace with the pressures of globalization.'' It inspects less than 1 percent of food shipments to the United States, and it admits that it would take nine years to inspect every high-priority, foreign pharmaceutical facility just once. Thus, consumers are left vulnerable and are forced to protect themselves. This can be achieved through the use of COOL where consumers can avoid products from countries with known safety issues.

Furthermore, consumers will pay more for products labeled ''Made in the USA.'' In a study by Colorado State University, 73 percent of consumers were willing to pay a 19 percent premium for USA-guaranteed steak, and a 24 percent premium for USA-guaranteed ground beef. Based on these findings, the University of Florida estimated that implementing COOL would increase annual profits by $900 million for the U.S. steak industry, and $3 billion for the U.S. ground beef industry.

Unfortunately, this issue increasingly affects my generation as the world becomes globalized, moving toward one market where supply chains are exceedingly complex. Additionally, we thrive on having immediate access to information so that we can express our preferences, such as not purchasing products from countries with safety concerns, environmental issues, or human rights violations. Consequently, processing must be clearly defined by law and all products, both foreign and domestic, must have COOL.

Thank you for your time.

[The prepared statement of Mr. D'Urso appears in the appendix.]

Representative SMITH. Thank you very much for your recommendations and insights as well, and again for, a couple of years ago, providing me with some insights that I had not been privy to, particularly about the origin of labeling.

Let me ask Ms. Lovera the first question, if I could. You talk about how the Bush administration pushed, as you put it, ''public blessing of chicken.'' Thankfully, Congress didn't go along with that. Then you talk about how President Obama met with Hu Jintao, and shortly after this USDA announced new steps to be taken to honor China's request to export chicken to the United States.

It was at that very meeting with Hu Jintao that I personally raised a number of concerns about Liu Xiaobo, the Nobel peace prize winner, which may seem like a disconnect at a hearing like this but it absolutely is connected because that's when Hu Jintao pretty much, and the President as well, just overlooked the whole human rights issue for the art of the deal, for more money and more trading, which if this was a democracy we'd all be breaking out the champagne bottle, but it's not.

So I'm wondering what came out of that. Is that what unleashed the current situation that we find ourselves in with the push to issue new regulations? It seems like that is pretty much in the very near future. What do all of you think about the denial of visas for our people to go there and do their due diligence to try to protect American consumers? I think that's in the theater of the absurd category, when someone going over there as part of a trade mission, and this is obviously a safety inspection mission, is precluded their ability to even be physically present.

Professor Kennedy, maybe you want to speak out a little bit further about this low-level contaminant issue, that you highlighted in your testimony? I think that's a really important issue that does not get the focus. I thank you for bringing that out in your testimony.

Ms. Lovera, you pointed out too about the infant formula, which I raised—we all have raised—for years. Three hundred thousand infants were sickened by melamine, 12,000 were hospitalized, and at least 6 children were dead. But very often with chemicals it's not just the acute, it's the longer term.

I wonder if anyone has tried to follow up on what happened to those 300,000 estimated children who were sickened, and especially those who were hospitalized. I mean, it seems to me that, again, underscoring the dangers here, it's not just short-term you get sick, you get salmonella or some other sickness. I've had it. I've had E. coli. It hurts you for 10 days and then you're better after a combination of antibiotics.

But some of these things obviously go deep into tissue and cause recurring, and maybe lifelong—we all know what mercury does. As you pointed out, the tilapia coming here—the number of pounds is huge. So if you could speak to some of those issues, and then I have some additional questions.

Ms. Lovera. Sure. So for the first question about the process and the timeline of events for China's system being declared equivalent, we have always been very concerned that this was less about the standards in their system being held up to the standards in our system than it was about opening this market.

In addition to the human rights issues that you've mentioned, which always seem to be a piece in the chess match of trade negotiations, we have been very concerned that this is happening at the same time that the U.S. beef industry is tremendously motivated to get the Chinese market opened to our beef, and we don't think that the timing is coincidental.

So this is what worries us, when trade trumps everything else. As we enter this next phase where the United States is negotiating new trade agreements, across both oceans with the TPP or the TTIP, this is what concerns us. These are trade agreements that are about reducing barriers to trade, which is fancy language for standards.

As consumers we need those standards. We need them to be set here, somewhere that's accountable to us as citizens. The Chinese food inspection system is not accountable to me as a U.S. citizen. I can't vote for them, I can't express that I think they're doing it wrong. We need to have confidence that we're using U.S. standards to judge what is safe to come in here and we worry a lot about that.

This is a perfect example of what happens when that gets put aside and it's more about moving product to a better market. On the visas issue, it concerns us greatly. We think that accessibility and the transparency of that system was an issue in figuring out the melamine situation. There was a delay. We don't think that we can respond, the United States can't respond, to track down problems if there's this kind of hold-up.

So again, it's a transparency issue and an accessibility issue about whether we're really going to be able to get there to figure out if there is a problem. On adulteration, with melamine as an example, this is something that folks who study China's food system bring up all the time. The jargon for it is economically motivated adulteration. The news media likes to call it food fraud.

I mean, whatever you call it, it's about substitutions that are cheaper and health is not being considered when the substitutions are being made, but you're vulnerable to that in a supply chain that is very long with a lot of middle men.

It was melamine in the milk powder, but then that got cracked down, but then we heard about some other product that was using scraps of leather, which has all kinds of metal contaminations, for derived protein, and you put that in the milk powders to try to beat the protein test. It just seems to be a recurring theme, in this market in particular. Substitutions that may not be safe do seem to be rampant and it's just one more reason we're very concerned about that being in the supply chain of food processors.

Representative SMITH. Professor?

Mr. KENNEDY. So first, relative to the point of visa denials to FDA, that is concerning that our officials are not able to get better access to these facilities. If you go back to the melamine contamination of wheat gluten that impacted pets here, the FDA was delayed in getting inspectors into China to take a look at the facilities involved because of just the relationship and the time required.

Actually, a firm that I'm familiar with was able to get their own people into that facility much earlier because they had people on the ground in China that were available to do that, and that's what the goal of having the offices in China is, to have that ready access and the ability to get into those facilities. That requires someone to have a visa in order for us to get in.

On the point about the process by which equivalency is being granted to China on processed poultry, and eventually being granted on poultry slaughter, as the Assistant Administrator outlined, this is basically a process that falls under our agreements with the WTO. So once we establish a specific food safety standard, we have to hold both foreign and domestic firms to that same standard.

So if we are not comfortable with how that standard is deployed overseas, we have to find a way to rewrite it so that it is applicable to both overseas and domestic firms and our comfort level with those organizations.

One of the challenges for doing the equivalency assessment is that it is a combination of a paperwork exercise and a limited amount of on-site inspection. So you go through a documentation review to make sure that the laws and regulations are the same as in their country as they are in our country, and that all of the requirements are the same.

Then you go into a limited set of audits to confirm that their practices are actually consistent with that. They are never surprise audits. They are always announced audits. So, yes, there is always the opportunity for the receiving country to decide that they are going to show you their best four plants and see if they can get that through. It's going to be true in any country but it's obviously a concern in a place like China.

But if we are not comfortable, we have to change how we regulate our own selves because it's going to change our status under the WTO if we make something more stringent for foreign manufacturers than we make it for ourselves.

If you go to the whole question about chronic toxicity and how that comes about, and what are the concerns there, if you go back to melamine contamination of pet food, the pet deaths were not because they consumed one bowl of the melamine-contaminated pet food and then got ill. They ate several, repeated doses of that material until they built up enough of the melamine to have melamine isocyanuric acid crystals accumulate in their kidneys and result in necrosis of the kidneys.

So that kind of chronic toxicity can be something that will present as an acute illness, but it's actually due to the chronic accumulation of that material over time. It is particularly troublesome for pets and children, as I mentioned in my longer testimony, because they eat the same thing every day. So if there's a low level of contamination that we don't understand, it can lead to these problems. That could be why this is taking so long to figure out because it's not anything we've ever looked at.

If you look at the report from FDA on what they've tested in the pet treats, it's probably the most expensive testing of contaminants in a food item that they've ever had to do and they still haven't figured out what it is because it's not something we're used to seeing. That's a continual problem.

The point was just raised by Ms. Lovera about economically motivated adulteration, and that is obviously an ongoing concern with China and has been for some time. Let me first remind everyone that economically motivated adulteration, or food fraud, is not new. It is as old as food.

The earliest food laws in Germany and in Egypt had to do with food fraud. Food fraud of protein products in the United States used to be a problem; it used to happen here, too. We substituted urea for protein in various products. So the Chinese are just going through a different series of substitutions a decade or two after we did the same thing.

Food fraud is considered to, by the Grocery Manufacturers Association, lead to $10 to $15 billion worth of economic loss to the food industry and may have up to 10 percent of food on shelf not being exactly as labeled. So consumers have the challenge of knowing what something is even when people are trying to do the right thing, but it's even more challenging when someone is not trying to do the right thing.

Then lastly on the whole question of the follow-up on China and the infant formula and what happened to those children over time, I'm not familiar with any studies that look at the long-term health effects of those original 300,000 children that were sickened in that event so I don't know if anything has been done there.

The only long-term exposure study that I'm aware of that has been done due to a food-borne illness contamination is actually related to an economically motivated adulteration of olive oil in Spain, which led to 700 deaths and thousands of chronic illnesses over time. That happened over 20 years ago and they're still monitoring the long-term health of those patients in that area of Spain, but that is only one of a large-scale contamination event that had chronic issues that I'm familiar with.

Representative SMITH. Mr. D'Urso, if I could ask you, as you testified, imported products that are processed in the United States are exempt from COOL. Who determines what constitutes processing, and can you explain how Customs and Border Protection and Agricultural Marketing Services define processing?

Mr. D'URSO. Sure. Unfortunately, the processing exemption is not something that is explicitly explained in the COOL laws, so it would be determined by the regulations of the enforcing agencies. Customs and Border Protection enforces the Tariff Act of 1930 aspect, which covers most imports. The Agricultural Marketing Service of the USDA enforces the Farm Bills of 2002 and 2008, which cover the agricultural commodities. Unfortunately, the two agencies have sometimes contradictory interpretations of the processing exemption, which leads to confusion and misinterpretation.

Customs and Border Protection defines processing as any method which results in the substantial transformation of a product whereby it experiences a change in name, character or use, where Agricultural Marketing Service defines processing as any type of cooking, curing, mixing, smoking, or restructuring, as in emulsifying.

Representative SMITH. So there are contradictions?

Mr. D'URSO. Yes, there are contradictions between the two.

Representative SMITH. In addition to the processing exemption, are there any areas of concern regarding COOL? As you testify before the Commission, do you have any suggestions or recommendations as to how to strengthen the COOL laws?

Mr. D'URSO. Absolutely. There are two other major issues where COOL laws need to be strengthened. First, companies oftentimes use catch-all labels whereby a multitude of possible countries of origin are listed, and this should not be allowed. Similar to lot numbers and expiration dates where they are specifically printed for a given production batch, the same should be required of country of origin so that there is no doubt as to the actual country of origin.

Second, as my generation becomes increasingly active with online shopping, online retailers in the United States should be required to disclose country of origin on the product listing Web page to inform consumers prior to purchase. Otherwise, consumers won't know country of origin until they receive the physical product.

And as for my recommendations with the specific COOL laws, first, the definition—the same definition—of processing should be explicitly stated in the respective COOL laws for both Customs and Border Protection and Agricultural Marketing Service so that it's not open to interpretation and there are no conflicts or contradictions.

In cases where production takes place in multiple countries, a product could be labeled as assembled in country X of components from country Y, or packaged in country X of components from country Y.

Second, products made in the United States should be required to have COOL in order to prevent confusion as to whether a product was made in the United States or imported and processed in the United States. Such labeling will provide consumers with confidence and transparency in the products they're purchasing so that they can make educated decisions.

Representative SMITH. Thank you.

Dr. Engeljohn mentioned that we rely on the government of China for so much of the information that we get, audits and the like, although we do our own, and that there's a 60-day lead time which is, as you Professor, just referenced in terms of advanced notice.

I mean, you can even reconstruct the whole thing if you wanted to in the 60-day lead time, it seems to me. And whistleblowers, which I asked about. I wonder if you have any thoughts, any of you, on the need to protect whistleblowers if they do exist in China with regard to this.

Ms. Lovera, you made a very important point about the school lunch program, to the maximum extent possible and the flexibility that local schools will have to buy things that have been made in China, chicken for example, that may be injurious to their students' health. How do we fix that?

Ms. LOVERA. Well, one thing that is extremely current is a provision in the House version of the agricultural appropriations for 2015 that would block importation of processed poultry for the school lunch program. It needs to be in the Senate version as well. It was, I think, the one thing they agreed on during that markup. But it's in the House version, so that's one particular piece of attention that's being paid to that school lunch issue.

We're asking school food service directors who are dealing with a thousand other things to deal with this. It's a hot topic around here right now about how much flexibility they get to meet nutrition requirements. They have a lot to do and now we're going to have to ask them, if we start importing this product, to be on the look-out for this on a vendor list or something like that and getting the product in and off the back of the truck, and then it has a Chinese label on it, isn't going to be super helpful. They need it up front. It's just another thing they have to deal with.

We don't think parents want this. There's a large petition, over 300,000 people, a bunch of groups have gathered this petition to say that people don't want this in school lunches. So I think it's a very fixable problem. That's a smaller scale. We would prefer USDA reevaluate the whole decision about bringing this product in, but at a minimum it doesn't belong in school lunches.

Representative SMITH. Thank you.

Mr. KENNEDY. So relative to the question of whistleblowers, I am similarly unaware of any particular whistleblower coming forward and reporting a problem in the food industry and there being any punishment or reward for that individual. There were bloggers related to the melamine incident. I do not know what happened to those bloggers in the melamine incident.

There have been a lot of people in China protesting the subsequent failures of the Chinese industry and Chinese Government to protect them from fraudulent business practices and food safety events, and there have been no public prosecutions of any of those people who have protested that I'm aware of, but I couldn't speak to that specifically.

Regarding the school lunch program, while many consumers obviously are concerned about the possibility of poultry from China ending up in the school lunch program, I think consumers would be surprised to realize that it's nearly impossible for us to have a school lunch program without some imported ingredients being used in that school lunch, and that there is a very high likelihood that some of those ingredients are from China already.

Given how we source some of our products globally, it's nearly impossible to eat a domestically-only sourced meal because there are some things that we simply don't produce. Even when we import it from countries we may think are more consistent with our own regulatory system, because of the way things are labeled by economic value, as Ms. Lovera has referred to, it is not always transparent as to where it really came from.

If you do a check on FATUS to see where we get citric acid from in the United States, we get it from China and we get it from Canada, 50 percent from China, 40 percent from Canada. Canada does not make citric acid, so we're getting Chinese citric acid through Canada.

So if we want country of origin labeling it actually has to be something that is the provenance of the supply chain owners because they're the only ones that have the visibility of the supply chain back far enough to say where they actually got something. When they do that, sometimes they can't definitively tell you what one batch was. If you buy something like chocolate, chocolate is intentionally commingled with cocoa beans from different sources to get a particular flavor profile.

They'll change that ratio based on the quality of the beans, so one day's production might have all four countries, one day's production might only have three countries. So it becomes complicated for companies to implement country of origin labeling unless they do a catchment of sources, we know it came from one of these four countries. But as Christopher D'Urso has said, some consumers will be frustrated by that.

The solution I put forth in my written testimony was that we have to look at something other than labeling on the package because you can't get that level of complexity on the label that firms would be able to deploy. We need to look at technology solutions so that we can provide Internet access to the information they need to know about the product. In using a lot-code basis to link to that data you could do that.

Representative SMITH. Thank you.

Thank you. I yield back.

Chairman BROWN [presiding]. Thank you, Mr. Smith. I appreciate that. I apologize again for having to have stepped out for half an hour.

So first of all, I wanted to thank Dr. Engeljohn who is still in the room. It is unfortunately all too unusual for administration representatives to stay and listen to a citizen's panel and we noticed, obviously. Or you look a lot like him, the guy that was sitting up here earlier. So thank you for that. Congressman Smith knows, too. It doesn't really matter, the political party, the administration doesn't do that enough. So, thank you for staying and listening to them.

I have in the last few minutes a question for two of you, starting with Mr. Kennedy. You mentioned, and I just heard you say kind of again in addition to your written testimony, that the hurdle of country of origin labeling is the scale and complexity of our entire food system with a single product, potentially including ingredients from many different countries. Your citric acid story was pretty interesting.

Given consumers' desire for this information, how do you propose a feasible way of providing sort of better, more complete, more reliable, and more honest information to consumers? How do we build that better?

Mr. KENNEDY. So again, I think it goes back to looking to a technology-based solution to enable the firms to provide that information in a reasonably accessible form that they can reasonably maintain. If you are going to ask them to put it on the label, the label would have to be printed uniquely for every batch. That becomes cost prohibitive.

They have to have some standards for labeling the rest of the material and labor, but more importantly if it is something that has 30, 40 ingredients, which many processed foods have, and those ingredients come from any one of 30 countries, where is the room on the label to actually list all of that in a way consumers could read it and utilize it?

Whereas if the production code was linked to a database that they could access online and say, this is where it's from. You do this with those QR codes now when you want to see what the reviews are of a product or other information.

So there are technology options that could make COOL more reasonably achievable and give consumers the level of information they want. At least the firms that I've talked with, their objection is not to wanting to make that information accessible to the public, it's that they don't always know how to do it if they have to put it on the label. It's simply a very significant logistic problem and the level of granularity will actually change how they have to process the foods in their system in order to comply. So it can be done.

For some foods it becomes very difficult, but because of that I think we have to look to non-traditional solutions such as creative use of technology solutions to enable firms to do so, and look at their ability to gain visibility in the supply chain to deal with these problems, and many others.

Chairman BROWN. Ms. Lovera, I don't think you entirely agree with that. Give me your thoughts.

Ms. LOVERA. We hear that a lot as a group that's worked on country of origin labeling for a long time, and there is a spectrum of how complicated foods are. We hear from folks that are producing single-ingredient foods that they can't figure out country of origin labeling, and that argument we don't buy. So we've seen the meat industry attack this concept since it came up over a decade ago. So, there are solutions that we can figure out.

If we're talking about the covered commodities that the Farm Bill language says that we have to label, ground beef was a sticking point for years and there was a compromise that was figured out. It doesn't get exactly where Christopher wants us to get but it says ''this may contain product from multiple countries'' because, whether or not consumers want to hear it, there may be lots of different animals in a vat or something that becomes ground beef, and it may come from multiple places, and that does shift.

So as a compromise, all sides, including folks who hated country of origin labeling and folks who wanted it, came to that compromise in the 2002 Farm Bill and said you can do a shotgun label as a way to move this process forward.

I do agree that we eat a lot of processed foods that have a long list of ingredients. My consumer advice to people is that if it has that many ingredients, maybe you don't need to eat it because you can't figure out where they all came from.

But if people are going to keep eating them and we're going to keep making them, we can at least start by giving a little bit more information on the package. So one proposal we are very interested in is something called ''In-By-For,'' like, this was made in this country by this company for this company, if it's a subcontracting type of arrangement, which is often hidden from consumers. We think that matters because those are often still sold under iconic American brands.

People may not realize that we've shifted that production to another country because it's cheaper, because it still says candy bar *X* that you used to buy when you were a kid when they made it in whatever State they made it in. So that's a start. They may not tell you where every coffee bean or piece of chocolate came from, but it could tell you who's doing it. That is a start and then we can get into other ideas about the various ingredients in a complicated processed food.

Chairman BROWN. Okay. That's very helpful, thank you.

We're going to wrap up. Before adjourning I want to enter into the record a letter of testimony submitted by Terry Safranek representing Animal Parents Against Pet Treats Made in China. She lives in Brooklyn Heights, Ohio, a suburb of Cleveland. Without objection, I'd enter this into the record. Thank you, Chairman Smith.

[The prepared statement of Ms. Sefranic appears in the appendix.]

Chairman BROWN. One comment and then I will close. This is incredible, just listening to any of the three of you or the other two, how complicated this is. If it's complicated to all of us who have actually put real time for a number of years into studying this, think how complicated it is obviously for American consumers. Ultimately when you think of a contaminated pharmaceutical and you think of the breadth and the depth and the reach of buying these products, and particularly, as Cochairman Smith said, in countries that are less than democracies or just countries that are so large there is no way to really inspect every little mom-and-pop operation making a pharmaceutical ingredient or contributing to the food supply. So then the cost to U.S. taxpayers when so much of the supply is so far flung around the globe, I know the solution to some is, with pet food, buy it if it says ''Made in the USA,'' although that doesn't always tell the whole story.

But I think it's also the question of responsibility, that those companies that move their production from here to abroad and then sell the products back into the United States because it saves them money should have ultimate responsibility for the products they're sending in, where they came from, where the ingredients came from, where they were assembled, where they were put together, and what happened as they were shipped back to the United States. So I thank the three of you, thank the two that testified before. If Chairman Smith or I have any written questions, or other members of the Commission do, please get responses to us within a week, if you would be willing to do that.

Commission adjourned. Thank you so much.

[Whereupon, at 5:37 p.m. the hearing was adjourned.]

APPENDIX

PREPARED STATEMENTS

PREPARED STATEMENT OF DANIEL L. ENGELJOHN

JUNE 17, 2014

Chairman Brown, Co-Chairman Smith, and members of the Commission, I am Dr. Dan Engeljohn, Assistant Administrator of USDA's Food Safety and Inspection Service's Office of Field Operations. I am pleased to appear before you today to explain the current state of U.S. regulatory oversight of poultry exported from the People's Republic of China (PRC) for human food.

OUR MISSION

First, let me take some time to explain FSIS's mandate. By law, FSIS is required to examine and inspect all slaughtered and processed livestock and poultry, as well as all processed egg products produced for use in commerce for human consumption. Our inspectors and veterinarians monitor the health of the animals brought to slaughter and ensure that livestock are treated humanely. These inspectors also collect the samples that our scientists analyze for the presence of pathogens and illegal drug residues. These dedicated men and women are on the front lines nationwide enforcing regulations and directives backed by scientific evidence to ensure that meat, poultry, and processed eggs in commerce are safe and wholesome.

FSIS also regulates all imported meat, poultry, and processed egg products intended for use as human food through a three part process:

• First, before FSIS-regulated products can enter the country, the agency determines whether the food safety regulatory system of any country that wishes to export to the United States is equivalent to our own system.
• Second, once FSIS finds a foreign country's food safety system to be equivalent, FSIS re-inspects eligible products from that country at U.S. ports-of-entry. During FY 2013, FSIS personnel inspected approximately 3 billion pounds of meat and poultry products presented for import by 28 actively exporting foreign countries, as well as about 10 million pounds of processed egg products.
• Third and finally, FSIS evaluates an exporting country's food safety system on an ongoing basis. Each year, FSIS reviews any changes in the foreign country's food safety system.

In addition, FSIS may conduct an in-country audit of the system and will review the country's performance in port-of-entry inspections. Based on these reviews, the Agency decides whether the country is maintaining equivalence, or whether additional Agency action is warranted. This performance-based approach allows FSIS to direct its resources to foreign food regulatory systems that potentially pose a risk to public health and makes our international program more consistent with the U.S. domestic inspection system. Our approach improves the linkage between port-of-entry re-inspection and on-site audits.

REGULATORY OVERSIGHT

Again, let me assure you that FSIS follows every mandate given the Agency to ensure that our food supply is safe. FSIS audits any foreign country that wishes to export meat, poultry, or processed egg products to the United States. A foreign country's inspection system must ensure that establishments preparing to export to the United States comply with requirements equivalent to those in the Federal Meat Inspection Act, the Poultry Products Inspection Act, the Egg Products Inspection Act, and in FSIS regulations. This is true for the PRC as it would be for any other country.

As you know, pursuant to requirements in the fiscal year 2010 Agriculture, Rural Development, Food and Drug Administration, and Related Agencies Appropriations Act (PL 111–80), the Agency is also required to provide Congress with detailed updates on China's request for equivalency every six months. However, let me explain briefly where we are in the process for the PRC—a process that began in 2004 with the PRC's request for on-site FSIS audits of its poultry processing and slaughter system.

• First, the United States is not importing any chicken that was slaughtered in China. A March 2013 audit found China's **poultry slaughter** system **not** equivalent to that in the United States; and
• Second, FSIS reaffirmed in August 2013 that the PRC's **poultry processing** inspection system is equivalent to that of the United States. This means that

chicken slaughtered in the U.S. or another country whose poultry slaughter system has been found by FSIS to be equivalent to the U.S. system could be sent to China for processing and then exported to the United States.

Again, the only chicken currently permitted to be imported from China is processed chicken from approved sources. FSIS, in coordination with USDA's Animal and Plant Health Inspection Service (APHIS), also currently requires that all processed chicken products from China be cooked.

China has provided a list of four plants it has certified as eligible to export processed chicken to the United States. Before any processed chicken can be exported to the United States, a proper export health certificate must be developed by the PRC and approved by FSIS and APHIS. Such a certificate, a draft of which was submitted earlier this month, must demonstrate that the poultry is sourced from the United States or from a country with an inspection system for slaughter that is equivalent to that of the United States and that the poultry was cooked to a proper temperature, among other things. Once FSIS and APHIS approve a certificate, and that certificate is agreed to by the PRC, the PRC will then be able to determine when to begin shipping products from the plants certified to export processed poultry products to the United States. The Agency doesn't have any information about how much processed product it expects China to ship once certification is up and running.

In addition to carrying a proper certificate, product must be properly labeled. Under Poultry Products Inspection Act regulations at 9 CFR 381.205, immediate containers of poultry products imported into the United States for human consumption must bear a label showing the name of the country of origin. Because processed product from China must be cooked, FSIS believes that it is unlikely that the product would be repacked or further processed in this country. If a product is not repacked or further processed, the label would indicate that the product is from the PRC. If the product were to be repacked or further processed in the United States at an official establishment, it would not include information that such product was from the PRC, but it would be repacked or processed under FSIS inspection. However, I would like to emphasize again that our systems-based approach to equivalence is designed to assure Americans that the food safety systems of other countries that FSIS finds to be equivalent, including the PRC's, are effective.

Of course, FSIS will also conduct annual on-site audits of the PRC's inspection system for processed poultry for at least the next 3 years, as we would do for any country that has just been found to be equivalent.

CONCLUSION

The dedicated men and women of FSIS work every day toward a common and extremely important goal of preventing food-borne illness. We take our mission seriously and understand the importance of our roles in ensuring the safety of the nation's food supply—whether from domestic or from foreign establishments.

Thank you for your continued support and the opportunity to report on the work we do to protect public health.

————

PREPARED STATEMENT OF TRACEY FORFA

JUNE 17, 2014

INTRODUCTION

Good afternoon, Chairman Brown, Co-Chairman Smith, and Members of the Commission. I am Tracey Forfa, Deputy Director of the Center for Veterinary Medicine (CVM) at the Food and Drug Administration (FDA or the Agency), which is part of the Department of Health and Human Services (HHS). Thank you for the opportunity to be here today to discuss FDA's investigation into reported illnesses in pets that consumed jerky pet treats.

FDA has been receiving reports of pet illnesses associated with the consumption of jerky pet treats since 2007. As of May 1, 2014, FDA has received approximately 4,800 such reports, including 1,800 complaints received since FDA's website update in October 2013. The reports received involve illnesses in more than 5,600 dogs, 24 cats, three humans, and, sadly, more than 1,000 canine deaths. Most of the reported cases involve chicken, duck, or sweet potato jerky products imported from China. Unfortunately, to date, FDA has not been able to identify a specific cause for the reported illnesses or deaths despite an intensive scientific investigation. Getting to the bottom of this problem is a priority for FDA, and the Agency is continuing its comprehensive investigation into the potential cause of the pet illnesses.

The ongoing global investigation is complex and includes a wide variety of experts at FDA, including toxicologists, epidemiologists, veterinary researchers, forensic chemists, microbiologists, field investigators, state research partners, and senior Agency officials. FDA has collaborated with our colleagues in academia and industry and has reached out to U.S. pet food firms to enlist their help and to share data involving this public health investigation. FDA is updating veterinarians and pet owners about the investigation regularly via the Agency's website and a webpage dedicated specifically to issues related to jerky treats. This information has been further disseminated to veterinarians by various groups, including the American Veterinary Medical Association (AVMA). Most recently, on May 16, 2014, CVM released an update entitled ''FDA Provides Latest Information on Jerky Pet Treat Investigation.'' CVM also has a webpage entitled ''FDA Progress Report on Ongoing Investigation into Jerky Pet Treats.'' In addition, the Agency will continue to remind pet owners that jerky pet treats are not necessary for pets to have a fully balanced diet, so eliminating them will not harm pets since commercially produced pet food contains all of the nutrients that pets need.

ADVERSE EVENT REPORTS

The 4,800 reports of pet illnesses received by FDA cover many sizes and ages of dogs, and multiple breeds. About 60 percent of the reports are for gastrointestinal illness and about 30 percent relate to kidney or urinary issues. Some dogs with kidney or urinary issues were diagnosed with Fanconi or Fanconi-like Syndrome, a rare kidney disease normally seen primarily in certain breeds as a genetic disease, although Fanconi can also be acquired following exposure to kidney toxins. Affected dogs were reported to involve a wide variety of breeds, which makes genetic Fanconi Syndrome unlikely. The background incidence of Fanconi Syndrome in dogs is currently unknown, but it appears to be increasingly reported in association with jerky treat ingestion. The remaining 10 percent of cases involve a variety of other symptoms, including convulsions, tremors, hives, and skin irritation.

In October 2013, FDA published an update on the Agency's website which resulted in a surge of 1,800 adverse event reports received by FDA. The Agency has determined that about 25 percent of the 1,800 reported cases were ''historic''; that is, the illnesses occurred several months or even years previously. The remaining cases were more recent, but may or may not have received veterinary attention. Of the new cases since October, the Agency has identified about 125 well-documented cases for further investigation, and has continued to correspond with the owners and veterinarians of these pets to track their progress and to obtain test samples of blood, urine, feces, and tissue.

In addition to the October 2013 website update, FDA reached out through the AVMA to solicit information about new or ongoing cases currently under veterinary care. This is a novel approach, and it resulted in the submission of tissue samples (blood, urine, feces, necropsy, etc.) from affected dogs that were associated with jerky pet treat exposure.

FDA has also had the opportunity to perform post-mortem examinations on dogs suspected of having jerky-pet-treat-associated illnesses. As of May 1, 2014, the Agency completed 26 post-mortems on the samples submitted since October 2013. In half of the cases, the dogs' cause of death was due to a variety of other causes, such as widespread cancer, trauma or infections; in the remaining 13 cases, 11 had kidney disease and two involved gastrointestinal disease. An exact causal relationship between these deaths and jerky pet treats has not been determined, but involvement of jerky pet treats has not been ruled out. We are exceptionally grateful to the owners who consented to allow FDA to perform post-mortem examinations of their beloved pets. We understand this is a difficult decision to make and sincerely appreciate the opportunity to learn more about the potential cause of their pets' deaths.

Beginning in May 2014, FDA has partnered with the Centers for Disease Control and Prevention (CDC) to collaborate on a study of cases reported to FDA of sick dogs compared with ''controls'' (dogs that have not been ill). The goal of the study is to compare the foods eaten by the sick dogs (cases) to those eaten by the dogs that did not get sick (controls), in order to determine whether sick dogs are eating more jerky pet treats than healthy dogs.

Investigators have identified about 100 cases of kidney illnesses in dogs reported to FDA to have occurred on or after July 1, 2013. The cases included dogs diagnosed with Fanconi or Fanconi-like illness, or dogs that were five years of age or younger and had kidney failure, regardless of jerky pet treat exposure. Cases were selected solely on this case definition and not on what food they consumed. Data collected during this investigation will allow Federal investigators to better understand what is making pets sick. The study is still ongoing, and FDA will share results when the study is completed.

Since 2011, in concert with FDA's Veterinary Laboratory Investigation and Response Network (Vet-LIRN), which partners with state and university veterinary diagnostic laboratories, the Agency has collected approximately 250 jerky treat samples related to more than 165 consumer-related complaints, plus more than 200 retail samples (unopened bags obtained from a store or shipment), and has performed more than 1,000 tests on these samples. In addition, the team at Vet-LIRN ran more than 240 tests on historical samples (those received in 2007–2011).

FDA's Vet-LIRN program has included intensive testing for numerous contaminants such as: *Salmonella;* metals or elements such as arsenic; pesticides; antibiotics; antivirals; mold and toxins from mold testing; rodenticides; nephrotoxins such as ethylene glycol and melamine; and other chemicals and poisonous compounds. FDA's test results of jerky treat product samples for toxic metals, including tests for heavy metals, have been negative.

Testing has also included measuring the composition of jerky pet treats to verify that they contain the ingredients listed on the label and do not contain ingredients that are not listed on the label. FDA is reaching out to private food testing laboratories for help with this work to better allow FDA to focus efforts on other aspects of the investigation. It is important to understand the composition of a product and its ingredients to determine where there might be a potential for problems to occur. For example, during a prior investigation involving contaminated pet food, FDA looked carefully at all the ingredients and it was later discovered that melamine was being used to raise the level of the protein in the products. Currently, FDA is investigating whether potentially contaminated glycerin could be a possible source of the reported illnesses in pets. FDA has tested a limited number of samples of glycerin obtained from inspections and is actively investigating new methodologies for analyzing glycerin for a variety of contaminants or impurities.

Testing of jerky pet treats from China has revealed the presence of the drug amantadine in some samples containing chicken. These samples were from jerky pet treats that were sold a year or more ago. Amantadine is an antiviral medication that is FDA-approved for use in humans. It has also been used in an extra-label manner (using an approved drug in a way that is not listed on the label) in dogs for pain control, but FDA prohibited its use in poultry in 2006.

FDA does not believe that amantadine contributed to the illnesses because the known side effects or adverse events associated with amantadine do not seem to correlate with the symptoms seen in the jerky-pet-treat-related cases. Amantadine, however, should not be present at all in jerky pet treats, and the Agency has notified the Chinese Administration of Quality Supervision, Inspection and Quarantine (AQSIQ) that the presence of amantadine in these products is an adulterant. Chinese authorities have assured FDA that they will perform additional screening and will follow up with jerky pet treat manufacturers. FDA has notified the U.S. companies that market jerky pet treats that were found positive for amantadine of this finding and is testing both imported and domestic jerky pet treats for amantadine and other antivirals. FDA is in the process of conducting a survey assignment of both domestic and imported jerky pet treats for amantadine, as well as other antivirals. Of the 41 samples analyzed thus far, only one has tested positive for antivirals.

FDA's testing also found various antibiotic residues in chicken jerky pet treats, which were also found by the N.Y. State Department of Agriculture and Markets. Though FDA does not believe the presence of these residues contributed to the reported illnesses in jerky pet treats, they should not be present in the products. These findings led to the temporary removal from the market of two major brands of jerky pet treats.

It was just over a year ago that FDA testified before this Commission about FDA's efforts to ensure global product safety and quality, particularly in our work related to China. China is the source of a large and growing volume of imported foods, drugs, and ingredients. Every product imported from abroad must meet the same standards as those produced here in the United States.

Firms always have the primary responsibility to produce safe products, but it is important that governments provide meaningful and robust regulation to ensure public safety. FDA is continuing its work with Chinese officials to help them improve their regulatory system and educate them on the new standards that are being implemented in our regulatory system.

FDA has held regular meetings with the Chinese authority, AQSIQ, about the jerky pet treat issue. These meetings have helped to ensure that AQSIQ is aware of U.S. requirements for pet food safety and to share information in support of FDA's investigation.

In April 2012, FDA conducted inspections of several facilities in China that manufacture jerky pet treats for export to the United States. FDA selected these firms for inspection because the jerky products they manufacture have been associated with some of the highest numbers of pet illness reports in the United States. These inspections provided valuable information on these firms' jerky pet treat manufacturing operations, including the ingredients and raw materials used in manufacturing, as well as manufacturing equipment, the heat treatment of products, packaging, quality control, sanitation, and product testing. Although these inspections helped to identify additional areas that FDA may investigate, the Agency found no evidence indicating that these firms' jerky pet treats are associated with pet illnesses in the United States. FDA, however, did identify concerns about the record keeping practices of several of the inspected Chinese firms. In particular, one firm falsified receiving documents for glycerin, which is a common ingredient in jerky pet treats. As a result of the inspection, the Chinese AQSIQ informed FDA that it had seized products at that firm and suspended exports of the firm's products to the United States.

As a follow-up to these inspections, FDA sent a delegation to China in April 2012 to express our concerns to AQSIQ about the complaints we continue to receive concerning jerky pet treat products imported from that country. As a result, FDA and AQSIQ agreed to expand the investigation of jerky pet treats. In addition to sharing our epidemiological findings with AQSIQ, FDA initiated a scientific collaboration, and has taken other steps to attempt to identify the root cause of the illness complaints. As noted, FDA and AQSIQ are meeting regularly to share findings and discuss further investigational approaches. FDA has also hosted Chinese scientists at the Agency's veterinary research facility to further scientific cooperation.

PET FOOD SAFETY IN GENERAL

Pet food safety in general continues to be a priority issue for FDA. In response to section 1002 of the Food and Drug Administration Amendments Act of 2007 (FDAAA), FDA established the Pet Food Early Warning Surveillance System. The goal of the surveillance system is to quickly identify contaminated pet food and illness outbreaks associated with pet food. The system uses data collected by two surveillance resources to collect information about pet-food-related problems: FDA's Consumer Complaint Reporting System (through the FDA District Consumer Complaint Coordinators) and the FDA-National Institutes of Health Safety Reporting Portal (SRP) (where consumers can submit complaints regarding adverse events in animals associated with the consumption of pet food). Information provided through these reporting mechanisms helps provide early detection of problems with pet food, enabling FDA to respond quickly to prevent or mitigate risks to people and animals.

The SRP launched in May 2010, allowing the public to submit complaints electronically. Using the portal's pet food questionnaire, consumers can report possible adverse health effects associated with their pets' food. Veterinarians may also report pet food safety problems on behalf of their clients and provide valuable medical information. Within days of opening the SRP for pet food complaints, veterinarians identified a thiamine deficiency in a cat that only ate one brand of canned food and reported it through the SRP. FDA notified the manufacturer, which promptly initiated a recall.

Another important safety surveillance tool is a new requirement, provided for in section 1005 of FDAAA, that manufacturers, processors, packers, and holders of human or animal food report to FDA if there is reasonable probability that an article of human or animal food will cause serious adverse health consequences or death to animals or humans. In conjunction with that requirement, section 1005 also required FDA to establish the Reportable Food Registry (RFR), an electronic portal to which such reports can be submitted. The intent of the registry is to help FDA better protect public health by tracking patterns of possible food and feed adulteration and to better target inspection resources. By providing early warning signals about potential health risks, it has increased the speed with which FDA, its state and local partners, and industry can remove hazards from the marketplace. For example, in 2011, a pet treat distribution company submitted a report to the RFR that their pig ear dog treats were contaminated with *Salmonella.* After FDA's investigation, two lots of the affected pet treats that had been distributed to 18 states were recalled.

In addition, FDA uses a system called the Pet Event Tracking Network (PETNet) to share information about emerging pet-food-related illnesses and product defects. PETNet is a secure network launched in August 2011 that allows the exchange of information between FDA and other Federal and state regulatory agencies. Using the shared information, state and Federal agencies can work together to quickly determine what regulatory actions are needed to prevent or quickly limit adverse effects associated with pet food products.

Finally, section 1002 of the FDAAA required FDA to establish processing standards for pet food. The process controls standards for pet food have been incorporated into the proposed rule, "Current Good Manufacturing Practice and Hazard Analysis and Risk-Based Preventive Controls for Food for Animals," which, when finalized, will implement, for animal food, section 103 of the FDA Food Safety Modernization Act. The proposed rule, which issued on October 25, 2013, establishes requirements for the safe manufacturing, processing, packing, and holding of animal food to protect animals and humans from foodborne illness.

CONCLUSION

Thank you for the opportunity to describe FDA's ongoing efforts to determine a definitive cause of the reported pet illnesses associated with jerky pet treats. The Agency is devoting significant resources to actively investigate the problem and its origin. FDA continues to work in collaboration with a wide variety of experts, including our colleagues in academia and industry, our international counterparts, and Federal, state and university laboratories, on this investigation. If FDA's investigation leads to the identification of any particular jerky pet treat ingredient or contaminant that is associated with illnesses in pets, the Agency intends to act quickly to notify the public of its findings and take steps, as appropriate, to ensure the affected product is promptly removed from the market.

FDA encourages consumers to check our website for updates on the ongoing investigation. As noted above, we will continue to remind pet owners that jerky pet treats are not necessary for a pet's healthy diet.

I am happy to answer any questions you may have.

PREPARED STATEMENT OF SHAUN KENNEDY

JUNE 17, 2014

Chairman Brown, Chairman Smith and distinguished members of the Commission, I would like to thank you for this opportunity to provide my perspective on current concerns with the safety of the food and feed system and potential steps to make it safer. I am the Director of the Food System Institute, LLC, a food system risk management and research firm and I have been focused on protecting our food system for years in prior positions as Director of the National Center for Food Protection and Defense, as Associate Professor of Food Systems in the Department of Veterinary Population Medicine at the University of Minnesota and as Vice President of Global Food and Beverage Research Development and Engineering for Ecolab.

As is often the case, there are a number of ongoing public and animal health concerns that are related to potential food and feed contamination. The pet deaths that appear to be attributable to jerky treats imported from China have raised concerns among many that we are exposed to unknown risks due to imported food products and food ingredients. The most commonly identified type of treats are chicken jerky treats, which may also raise concern that the USDA's designation of China as an "equal to" country for processed poultry will expose consumers to additional unknown risks. The potential that the ongoing Porcine Epidemic Diarrhea virus (PEDv) outbreak in swine may be attributable, at least in part, to feed is another example of uncertain risk from food and feed. Among many possible solutions to these, and other, food system concerns are demands for increased regulatory inspection and clearer source labeling on consumers' packages, more commonly known as COOL or Country Of Origin Labeling. Before addressing either of those approaches, I would first like to provide a bit of context around our current food and agriculture system and what that implies for how either increased inspection or COOL could be effectively implemented.

Everyone realizes that we are sustained by a global food and agriculture system, but it is often hard to conceptualize how global it really is. In the first four months of this year, January through April, we imported food and raw agricultural products from more than 179 countries with a total value of over $48 billion and weighing over 26 million metric tons. When we focus on food items classified as "consumer oriented", which are products close to the form in which consumers would purchase them and not intermediate products like raw cocoa beans, we imported $23.5 billion and nearly 11 million metric tons of these products in the same four months. That is roughly 75 pounds per person in the U.S. for the first four months of the year or over half a pound per day. So at a basic level, we are always eating foods that come from around the world as well as those from around the block, and that is something that has been steadily growing over the last decade. In 2004, our imports of "consumer oriented" products were only $12 billion and 8 million tons or about 56 pounds per person in the first four months of the year. Those imports come from a broad range of facilities, with over 6,800 USDA–FSIS approved domestic facilities and over 250 approved foreign facilities while over 81,000 domestic and 115,000 firms are registered with the FDA to supply food to the U.S.

A significant challenge any consumer faces is figuring out the origin of each ingredient in any particular meal, but it is easier to understand where it could have come from. If your lunch today was a cheeseburger, French fries and milk, the last two are fairly straightforward. We are a big producer of both fluid milk and frozen French fries, with only five countries exporting frozen French fries to the US and five countries exporting fluid milk. In both cases the dominant source is Canada. That doesn't necessarily mean that all components of these food items are domestically sourced, however, as Canada, Chile and Mexico have historically been exporters of salt to the U.S. that may be on the French Fries and the vitamins added to the milk are primarily imported from China and a few other countries. The cheeseburger is a bit more complicated as the bun, burger, cheese, tomato, lettuce, pickle, onion, ketchup, mustard and seasoning, ten consumer level items, can contain 75 or more individual ingredients. Last year those ingredients were imported to some degree from over 55 countries. That means that, including domestic sourcing, the burger has billions of possible combinations of country of origin for its various ingredients.

While any specific burger obviously has a dramatically smaller range of sourcing options, this simple lunch illustrates both the complexity of the food system and the hurdles of country of origin labeling. If it is winter, the lettuce and tomato are usually imported from Mexico and Central America. The ground beef is often a mix of domestic and imported sources, from Australia and other sources, to meet quality demands. The bun, ketchup, mustard and seasoning usually include imported ingredients from a number of countries, especially since many spices don't grow in our climate. While a company could verify what the country of origin was for each ingredient, under COOL the challenge becomes how to label and where to put this information? This is further complicated by the fact that sources, especially for seasonal ingredients, may change several times a year. Ingredients may also be comingled in entirely different ways in a relatively short time frame based on availability, cost or quality parameters. Clearly, accurate and informative labeling on country of origin is thus a challenge. With the increasing use of web based solutions, the only reasonable option might be to provide the information in something like a QR Code that you see on many consumer products that would take the consumer to a website for details that cannot be reasonably provided on the label. Whatever the solution, including the potential of reducing sourcing complexity to make COOL more easily achievable, there is an additional expense that would have to be added to the retail cost of the product, and consumers will ultimately bear the burden of the increased cost of foods reaching their table.

The scale and complexity of the food system we depend on contributes significantly to the challenge of ensuring that our food is always safe and complicates our ability to rapidly figure out what has happened when something goes wrong. The pet deaths linked to pet treats from China illustrate these challenges. As a happy "parent" of Storm, an Aussie-doodle, the pet treat related deaths are personally troubling. Storm gets a little treat after our walk every night, so I have been following this ongoing concern closely. While the first cases were reported in 2007, no causative agent has yet been identified. This is even though FDA has conducted extensive testing of a broad range of treats, including treats provided by owners of pets who passed away, and no probable agent has been found. Without knowing what is causing the illnesses, and thus no means of screening products to ensure that they are safe, firms and authorities have limited options. Purina has moved to a dedicated, direct supply chain in China for its production of chicken pet treats. By controlling all aspects of production from hatching through slaughter and processing, Purina can better ensure the integrity and safety of their Chinese sourced chicken pet treats. Until we know what the cause of illness is, however, they don't have total assurance that this intensive effort has eliminated the potential for further illnesses.

If the problem is a low-level contaminant where cumulative dose is the reason for the illnesses, it could unfortunately take much more time to figure out. There are more unknowns and uncertainties with respect to chronic versus acute toxicities, whether the food is intended for human or animal consumption. Chronic toxicity becomes even more important for both infants and pets who tend to have the same limited sets of foods over time so that a low level of contamination in the treats, something not considered an acute health risk, could lead to chronic illness with the steady dose of treats over time. Additionally, pets and infants also consume more food per pound of body weight than adults and often have a lower threshold for illness than adults.

Regardless of whether the cause of illness was known, inspection and testing have limited utility in protecting public health for contaminants that are low-level and sporadic. Regulatory inspections and vendor audits have many benefits, including ensuring that the food safety system design meets regulatory or customer requirements. Inspections and audits also provide an awareness and education opportunity for all involved. They do not, however, provide an assurance of no probability of foodborne illness. If that were the case, there would never be an outbreak related to USDA inspected facilities since they have inspectors on site every day. In order to make sure that there are no deviations that could possibly lead to illness, it would require 100% inspection of every step from farm to table, and that is simply not achievable. Under the Food Safety Modernization Act (FSMA) the requirement is to inspect high-risk facilities at least every three years and other facilities every five years, and that is already well beyond the resources currently available to FDA. That is in part why third party audits are part of the FSMA framework, but even an annual inspection doesn't ensure that any individual food is safe.

Similarly, for product testing to provide 100% assurance of no contamination would require testing of all servings of the product, leaving very little to actually eat. That is not to say that product testing isn't an important part of an effective food safety plan. Product testing provides a means of monitoring the food safety system to ensure that it is under control. The first step, however, is to know what to test for, and in the case of the pet treats that is still an unknown. Once you know what to test for, such as Salmonella in a meat or poultry product, you have to decide how you will test and what your sampling strategy will be. For example, for ready-to-cook poultry products the USDA requirement involves one sample per day over a fixed period of time period where an acceptable level is determined by having a prevalence of positive samples less than a predetermined performance standard. This testing approach can potentially be improved by quantifying the amount of contaminant in the product. This enumeration approach adds value because toxicity or infectivity is based on ingestion of a sufficient dose of pathogen. Consequently, knowing that one source or point in the system has infrequent, but significant or high level contamination can be far more valuable than knowing that all sources or points have low, infrequent contamination. This is especially the case for ready-to-cook products where some level of foodborne illness organisms is acceptable.

Since the pet treats of concern are sourced from China there is heightened concern about the granting of "equal to" status for processed poultry from China that was approved last year. It is important to recognize that this was not a capricious decision by USDA, but instead the next step in a process that began a decade ago. Under the provisions of the World Trade Organization, a country can require any scientifically justifiable safety standards to protect its public so long as the requirements are equivalent for domestic and foreign firms. That is precisely what USDA has done, and it is why poultry slaughter in China is not yet granted "equal to" status as the Chinese regulatory system and facilities have not yet been found to be "equal to" those in the U.S. That does not mean that consumers are going to be exposed to dramatically new foodborne illness threats when processed poultry from China begins arriving in the U.S. In the last four years there have been five multi-state foodborne illness outbreaks associated with U.S. poultry, so there is already some level of foodborne illness risk associated with poultry. I can tell you that one of the absolute best poultry plants I have every conducted an audit on was in China. That facility's food safety system was driven more by its company's standards and customer expectations than any regulatory requirements, and that is very common both domestically and overseas. While there may be some baseline risk of illness due to consumption of food from any of the more than 179 countries we import food from, as was the case for that Chinese poultry facility, the real answer lies in the specific food systems and how they are managed. That is one of the strong points of FSMA as it will require firms to ensure that their suppliers, wherever they are, are meeting FDA requirements and thus some level of importer/supplier information sharing, directly or through the exporter, will have to occur. In addition, firms need to go beyond that minimum to certify that their suppliers meet the unique requirements of the intended finished product, and most firms already do that.

A different type of food and feed safety concern has been raised by the ongoing Porcine Epidemic Diarrhea Virus (PEDv) outbreak in the swine industry. Rabobank, a leading banking and financial firm focused on food and agriculture, has estimated that PEDv has impacted 60% of the U.S. sow heard and may reduce pork production by up to 7%. This would be the lowest pork production in the U.S. in over 30 years. While the pathway for PEDv spread to farms has not been confirmed, feed, or how the feed gets to the farm, has been strongly implicated. Swine transportation vehicles have also been identified as a potential source. Testing to date, however, has not been able to confirm that PEDv contaminated feed has been the source of any specific outbreak or that there is broad contamination of feed or feed ingredients with PEDv. This situation further illustrates the challenges of both testing as an intervention strategy and the current feed system complexity. Unlike the pet treat problem, with PEDv it is not just the animal that eats the feed that will get sick. Since an individual pig that gets ill can further spread the disease to others in its herd, it only takes a fraction of a herd to initially contract the virus for it to infect a large portion of the herd. Given that PEDv has a relatively low infective dose, it would thus only require low level, sporadic contamination of the feed, a feed ingredient or its packaging to spread the virus broadly. So even a robust testing strategy that was capable of detecting live virus at a very low level of every batch of feed could not match the effective sampling strategy of then providing the feed to tens of thousands of pigs where only a few of the servings would have to be contaminated for the virus to spread.

Whether the source is a feed ingredient or ingredient packaging, finished feed or transportation of feed to farm that turns out to be the source of the outbreak, the scale and complexity of the feed system makes solving the problem a challenge. For example, there are over 1,140 production-animal feed mills in the country so if the source is a feed ingredient, following a particular ingredient from its production to consumption and then matching that to geographic patterns of illness becomes very complicated. Just as is the case for almost every other final food product, there is no one place where all of the information on how the global food and agriculture system puzzle pieces fit together is maintained. Through their agreements with their suppliers, however, firms are in the best position to do this for their own products, regardless of what country they or their suppliers are located in. Supply chain visibility then becomes part of a firm's PEDv mitigation strategy.

To summarize, the ongoing association of pet deaths with Chinese sourced animal treats is understandably raising concerns. Until the actual cause of the illnesses is understood, however, inspections upon import or product recalls provide no assurance of greater safety. Even when the source is understood, it will likely still be more effective for firms to manage their supply chains to mitigate continued exposure than to expect import testing to prevent entry of any possibly contaminated treats. While there are many who are concerned about the prospect of allowing poultry processed in China to gain entry into the U.S. market, the approval is fully consistent with the current laws, regulations and international agreements. There are already some very good poultry production facilities in China, so, as is the case for domestic sourcing, with appropriate due diligence importers will have the ability to maintain the safety of their poultry products sourced in China. For both domestically produced and foreign sourced poultry, especially ready to cook poultry, the food safety system could be further strengthened by including enumeration of potentially pathogenic bacteria to the current prevalence approach. If the feed system is proven to be the means by which PEDv is spread to swine herds, sampling and testing of feed and feed ingredients will be a necessary but insufficient means of protecting the swine industry. Testing can provide assurances that the system is behaving as intended, but first the system has to be designed so that the potential for contamination has been mitigated in the first place. In each case, a firm's supply chain visibility is an important part of the food and feed safety strategy.

Ensuring that our food safety standards are met at every step from farm to consumer, pet or farm animal in the global food and agriculture system is a daunting challenge. While the enabling laws and regulations are different between the agencies within a country and between countries, they share to basic goal of preventing illness. On a day-to-day basis the responsibility of achieving that goal is taken up primarily by the firms themselves, with the oversight and support of their local regulatory authorities, as they have the visibility and control of their supply chain and facilities to do so. While overall the food and agriculture system does a remarkable job of safely feeding us, we should do better. Through effective partnerships across stakeholders, from industry to authorities to the research community, the encouraging thing is we can.

———

Testimony before the
U.S. Congressional-Executive Commission on China

Pet Treats and Processed Chicken from China:
Concerns for American Consumers and Pets

Patty Lovera
Assistant Director
Food & Water Watch

My name is Patty Lovera, and I am the assistant director of Food & Water Watch, a nonprofit consumer advocacy organization. Thank you for the opportunity to present testimony on this important topic.

Introduction

The United States is increasingly reliant on imported food. The U.S. Government Accountability Office (GAO) reports that from 2000 through 2011, the percentage of food consumed in the United States that was imported rose from 9 percent to over 16 percent, and food imports increased by an average of 10 percent each year for seven years.[1]

China is a growing supplier of the United State's food imports. China is the largest agricultural economy in the world and one of the biggest agricultural exporters.[2] It is the world's leading producer of many foods Americans eat: apples, tomatoes, peaches, potatoes, garlic, sweet potatoes, pears, peas — the list goes on and on.[3] It is also a leading producer of many of the inputs used to make processed food, for example ascorbic acid, or vitamin C, producing about 80 percent of the world supply.[4]

But the poorly controlled expansion of China's economy has often been fueled by excess pollution, treacherous working conditions, and dangerous foods and products that pose significant risks to consumers in China and worldwide. China is often described as home to a Wild West business environment that allows food manufacturers and processors to cut corners, sell tainted food products and rely on adulteration to maximize their competitive advantage.

Food safety problems in China have been making headlines around the world for quite a while, especially after several rounds of publicity concerning contamination of foods with a chemical, normally used to make plastic, called melamine. The chemical has been intentionally added to different food products in China, usually to try to artificially increase the nitrogen content in attempt to pass tests for protein levels.

In 2007, the U.S. Food and Drug Administration (FDA) received reports of 17,000 pet illnesses, including 4,000 dog and cat deaths, believed to be the result of melamine contamination in imported Chinese gluten used to make pet food.[5] Sixty million packages of pet food were recalled in the United States.[6] The potential health impacts were not necessarily limited to pet food, however, because some of the melamine-contaminated pet food was redirected to hog farms. Thousands of hogs that ate the contaminated food were put to death in an effort to keep melamine-contaminated meat from entering the food supply.[7] But the FDA and USDA still allowed 56,000 hogs that ate melamine-tainted pet food to be processed into pork, which was then sold at supermarkets.[8]

By 2008, the FDA had identified melamine in imported wheat gluten and rice protein from China (used in pet food), prompting rejections of 44 percent and 32 percent of these products, respectively.[9] While the FDA stopped these shipments, pet food imports from China continued to rise and reached 79 million pounds in 2010.[10]

Pet food turned out to be only the tip of the melamine iceberg. Because melamine was widely used in China to adulterate dairy products such as milk powder, processed food products including candy, hot cocoa, flavored drinks and, most tragically, infant formula contained the chemical.[11] An infant formula scandal erupted just before the 2008 Beijing Olympics and ultimately an estimated 300,000 infants and children in China were sickened by melamine; more than 12,000 were hospitalized.[12] At least six children died.[13]

While the melamine crisis may be the most widely covered Chinese food safety scandal, unfortunately it was not an isolated incident. International media sources routinely cover food safety problems originating in China, ranging from widespread smuggling of products like honey to avoid tariffs and food safety restrictions,[14] mislabeled products "transshipped" through another country but produced in China,[15] and importing countries discovering violations of pesticide or other food safety regulations.

A 2013 report by a food industry analyst found that among reported food violations in Chinese products, the most frequent cause was pesticides, followed by pathogen contamination. The report cited 32 pesticides found in laboratory testing of Chinese foods, mostly in produce, fruit and spices and noted that "economically motivated adulteration" is a persistent issue in food production in China.[16]

U.S. Food Imports From China

After joining the World Trade Organization in 2001, China's food exports to the United States tripled to 4.1 billion pounds of food in 2012.[17] In addition to Chinese firms exporting to the United States, U.S. food and agribusiness companies have capitalized on China's cheap labor costs and weak regulations, hoping to sell to a growing class of Chinese consumers and export to the United States.

The millions of pounds of imports from China represent a considerable portion of the food eaten by U.S. consumers. For example, in 2011:

- Eighty percent of the tilapia Americans ate came from the 382.2 million pounds of imports from China.
- The United States imported 367 million gallons of apple juice from China, amounting to almost half (49.6 percent) of U.S. consumption.
- The 70.7 million pounds of cod imported from China amounted to just more than half (51 percent) of U.S. consumption.
- The 217.5 million pounds of imported garlic was 31.3 percent of U.S. consumption.
- The 39.3 million pounds of frozen spinach represented 11 percent of U.S. consumption.

Other Chinese exports include processed foods and food ingredients, products which most consumers purchase without considering where they came from. China is a leading supplier to the United States of ingredients like xylitol, used as a sweetener in candy, and sorbic acid, a preservative.[18] China supplies around 85 percent of U.S. imports of artificial vanilla, as well as many vitamins that are frequently added to food products, like folic acid and thiamine.[19] By 2007, 90 percent of America's vitamin C supplements came from China, and by 2010, China supplied the United States with 88 million pounds of candy.[20] The United States also imported 102 million pounds of sauces, including soy sauce; 81 million pounds of spices; 79 million pounds of dog and cat food; and 41 million pounds of pasta and baked goods from China in 2010.[21]

China's Food Safety System

Chinese officials have readily acknowledged the country's food system as "grim."[22] The country's decentralized and overlapping regulatory system has not been able to address China's sprawling food-processing industry. Repeated government efforts to reform food safety rules have so far failed to stem the tide of adulterated food. After a major food safety law from 2009 went into effect, a professor at the Chinese Academy of Governance stated that poor coordination between agencies, lackluster enforcement and inadequate government oversight hindered the enforcement of food safety laws.[23] It remains to be seen if an overhaul of the food safety system, announced in 2012, will manage to coordinate efforts government-wide and tighten food safety standards.[24]

Reports on food safety problems since 2009 yield a long list of problems in both the domestic food supply and exported products. One persistent trend is "economically motivated adulteration," or what has been described as a culture of adulteration in China's agricultural sector.[25] Melamine contamination in Chinese food continues to be a problem, with a crackdown on melamine in milk powder in 2010 resulting in 96 arrests and 26 public officials being fired[26] and U.S. regulators finding high levels of melamine in a dog food shipment in January 2011.[27] After increased attention to the problem of melamine, some Chinese dairy producers appear to have switched to a new protein adulterant that is even more difficult to detect — hydrolyzed leather protein made from scraps of animal skin.[28]

Even veterinary drugs banned in China — such as clenbuterol, administered to animals to give them leaner meat and pinker skin — remain widely used in China despite years of documented consumer illnesses from residues in meat and organs,[29] and controversies over athletes avoiding meat for fear of testing positive for the performance enhancing drug.

Since 2009, the Chinese government has made a point of making public displays of enforcing food safety rules, inspecting food facilities and punishing people connected with tainted food. News reports frequently reference millions of inspections of facilities and frequent "crackdowns" on particular products. A search of news reports reveals a variety of enforcement efforts:

- The scandal over melamine-contaminated infant formula led to the execution of two people and prison terms for dairy company executives. [30]
- In 2011, industry and commerce authorities reported 62,000 cases of substandard food, leading to 43,000 unlicensed operations being shut down and 251 cases being sent to the judicial system. [31]
- A 2011 crackdown on food safety violations resulted in 2,000 arrests and 4,900 businesses being closed.[32]
- The Chinese news agency Xinhua reported in June 2012 that authorities shut down 5,700 unlicensed food businesses and discovered 15,000 cases of "substandard food" so far that year.[33]
- In early May 2013, news reports described a Chinese government campaign to break up a fake meat operation, leading to arrests of more than 900 people accused of passing off more than $1 million of rat meat as mutton.[34]

Ironically, the discovery of thousands of dead pigs in the Huangpu River was actually described in some media reports as "an encouraging step forward in Chinese public health," because it indicated that rather than sell diseased animals into the food supply, producers dumped them into the river instead.[35]

But despite the concerted effort to show that the government is tough on food safety violators, problems persist. A small sample of food safety problems:

- In 2010, a scandal erupted over the use of food coloring and bleach to plump up shriveled old peas so they would appear fresh.[36]
- Authorities detected plasticizers, chemicals linked to immune and reproductive system damage, in samples of a leading brand of distilled white liquor.[37]
- Testing by Greenpeace of 18 varieties of tea found that every sample contained at least three different kinds of pesticides. 12 of the samples showed traces of banned pesticides.[38]
- In September 2012, FDA refused 10 shipments of canned mushrooms from China due to pesticide contamination, resulting in the Chinese government halting exports of canned mushrooms to the United States.[39]

- China Central Television reported in 2012 that testing of preserved fruit from 16 different companies found excessive pigments, bleaching agents and preservatives, as well as incorrect expiration dates.[40]
- The Xinhua News Agency reported in 2012 that wholesale vegetable dealers in Shandong province were found spraying cabbages with formaldehyde, presumably to preserve them during transport without refrigeration.[41]
- A 2012 report noted that fish vendors in Beijing were using a chemical used for temporary dental fillings to tranquilize fish during transport. [42]
- In May 2013, officials in Guangdong Province, announced excessive levels of cadmium in over 100 batches of rice.[43]
- In December 2013, a Chinese government official announced that eight million acres of farmland in China was so polluted that it should not be used for growing crops.[44]
- Five strains of avian influenza have emerged in China in the last 17 years. In 2013, China had 115 human highly pathogenic avian flu cases in humans, including 25 deaths.[45]

Chinese consumers are not confident about their domestic food supply. A 2011 survey found that food safety is a major concern for almost 70 percent of Chinese consumers,[46] and there are regular reports of Chinese tourists emptying store shelves in other countries in search of infant formula not produced in China.

Another recurring theme is lack of transparency. China's food safety enforcement system lacks the transparency necessary to warn the public about dangerous products or deter dangerous food-processing practices. The USDA reports that the Chinese government zealously guards the food safety data it collects, making it difficult to impartially evaluate China's food safety performance.[47] In 2010, some officials criticized regional authorities that publicized a widespread case of pesticide adulteration rather than obeying the "unspoken rule" of keeping food safety problems hidden from the public.[48] The father of one child sickened by melamine-tainted milk powder was jailed, and eventually paroled, for his activism on the issue.[49]

U.S. Regulation of Chinese Food Imports

U.S. oversight of Chinese food processors has not remotely kept pace with the growth in imports. Though the Food and Drug Administration prevented 9,000 unsafe Chinese products from entering the country between 2006 and 2010,[50] it is not because of vigilant inspection at U.S borders and ports. The agency's low inspection rate — less than 2 percent of imported produce, processed food and seafood[51] — almost guarantees that unsafe Chinese products are making their way into American grocery stores.

Other importers of food from China have instituted more intensive testing regimes for Chinese imports. From 2004 to 2009, Japan tested between 15 and 18 percent of food products from China, and up to 38 percent of frozen vegetables.[52]

In 2007, the FDA's director of the Center for Food Safety and Applied Nutrition stated that the growing Chinese food exports have "outstretched and outgrown the regulatory system for imports in the U.S."[53] During the melamine-tainted pet food crisis, it took the FDA one month to even identify their regulatory counterparts in China.[54]

In 2007, China consented to allow FDA inspectors to be stationed in China, and the FDA opened its first office in 2008.[55] However, the few FDA inspectors in China were overwhelmed by the sheer size of the nation's food production, including an estimated 1 million food-processing companies.[56] Between 2001 and 2008, the FDA inspected 46 food firms in China — less than six a year.[57] After the spate of import scandals, the FDA increased inspections, but still only conducted 13 food inspections in China from June 2009 to June 2010.[58] In fiscal year 2012, FDA conducted 10 inspections of food facilities in China.[59]

Meat and poultry imports are the responsibility of the U.S. Department of Agriculture. Until 2009, FSIS conducted in-depth annual on-site audits of countries eligible to export meat, poultry and egg products to the United States. The department recently announced that in 2009 it made a major change to this system by ending annual visits to exporting countries, and instead starting to rely on a "Self-Reporting Tool" for countries as a substitute to annual audit visits. With this change, USDA began conducting audit visits every three years instead of annually and the agency stopped the practice of publishing the audit results of individual foreign meat, poultry, egg plants that exported products to the United States.

Poultry

The USDA's approach to China's interest in exporting poultry products to the United States offers a telling example of how the pressure to increase trade can leave food safety concerns as a lower priority. Currently, the United States does not import poultry for human consumption from China. U.S. agribusinesses have invested heavily in Chinese chicken production and processing – both to feed Chinese consumers and as a future export platform to U.S. consumers – and they have been working to get USDA approval for Chinese poultry exports to the United States.

In 2006, the USDA rapidly finalized China's request to begin exporting processed chicken to the United States the very same day as a visit from China's president.[60] This action apparently prompted China to resume negotiations over lifting its ban on American beef, instituted in 2003 after the discovery of mad cow disease in the state of Washington.[61]

Despite the Bush Administration's public blessing of Chinese chicken, the USDA's internal inspection reports of Chinese poultry facilities showed egregious food safety problems, including mishandling raw chicken throughout the processing areas, failing to perform *E. coli* and *Salmonella* testing, and routinely using dirty tools and equipment.[62] As these internal reports emerged, Congress refused to implement the Bush Administration proposal, effectively maintaining a ban on Chinese poultry imports.[63]

China contended the U.S. prohibition against its chicken, produced in unsafe plants with insufficient inspection, was an illegal trade barrier. The World Trade Organization agreed in September 2010.[64] The same month, China announced it would impose high tariffs on American chicken products for allegedly being priced too cheaply.[65]

In January 2011, Chinese President Hu Jintao again visited the United States, cementing tens of billion of dollars in trade deals with the Obama Administration.[66] Shortly after this visit, the USDA announced new steps it had taken to honor China's request to export chicken to the United States.[67]

Currently, the USDA's Food Safety and Inspection Service is working through the steps to approve China as an exporter of poultry products to the United States. In August 2013, USDA declared that the Chinese government's inspection system for poultry processing plants was equivalent to USDA inspection, thereby clearing the way for certain chicken processing facilities in China to be able to export poultry products to the United States.[68] The Chinese government must certify plants that are eligible to export to the United States before shipments can begin.

In December 2013, USDA stated that China's inspection system for poultry slaughter is not equivalent to USDA inspection.[69] But it is widely believed that the ultimate goal of the poultry industry is to have this equivalence determination made so that products from Chinese-origin birds can be exported to the United States.

The processed poultry products that could eventually arrive in the United States are supposed to be made in Chinese plants from birds that have been sent from "approved" sources, including the United States or Canada, but not China. But without stationing USDA inspectors in Chinese processing plants, it will be virtually impossible to verify that these products are made from birds from approved sources rather than Chinese producers.

There are also concerns about the potential for processed poultry products from China to end up in school cafeterias. While the USDA's National School Lunch Program does source domestic product, most schools also procure food from private vendors. These purchases are supposed to source domestic product "to the maximum extent possible." In addition to cost pressure that could drive school systems to source Chinese processed poultry, the definition used to define U.S. product for school lunches also presents a pathway for Chinese processed poultry to end up in schools. Because the school lunch standard for a U.S. product is that at least 51 percent of the product must be domestic, a processed food item that contains chicken as well as other ingredients could contain Chinese-processed poultry and still meet the definition of a U.S. product.[70]

The FY 2015 agriculture appropriations bill being considered by the House of Representatives currently includes a prohibition on purchase of Chinese-processed poultry products for any of the USDA's nutrition programs. This follows widespread public opposition to the idea of importing poultry products from China, including a petition signed by over 300,000 people urging Congress to prevent chicken products from China from reaching U.S. supermarket shelves or school cafeterias.[71]

Pet Treats

The FDA reports "from 2003, when China first approached the USDA about poultry exports, to 2011, the volume of pet food exports (regulated by the FDA) to the United States from China has grown 85-fold."[72]

Since 2007, thousands of American dogs have fallen ill or died after eating chicken jerky treats made in China. In August 2012, four months after visiting Chinese processing plants that export pet treats to the United States, the FDA published inspection reports that revealed that the factories refused to allow U.S. inspectors to collect samples for independent analysis.[73] Ultimately, testing done by the New York Department of Agriculture and Markets found contamination of some of the treats with residues of an undisclosed antibiotic, triggering voluntary recalls of the products by the manufacturers.[74]

Just last month, the FDA released an update on this continuing health threat to U.S. pets. As of May 16, 2014, the agency had received 4800 reports of illnesses, involving 5600 dogs, 24 cats, and three people, and over 1000 canine deaths linked to consumption of jerky pet treats from China. The most common problems reported were gastrointestinal illness and kidney problems.[75]

Despite the long-running investigation and growing public awareness of this problem, the FDA has still not identified a cause for the illnesses and deaths. Recently, some observers of global food industry have urged the FDA to look not only at finished products, but also further up the supply chain of ingredients. In particular, they cited the possibility that leather-processing byproducts, often tainted with chromium, were being used to extract proteins that are added to poultry feed.[76]

While two major producers of chicken jerky treats did announce a voluntary recall of their products in early 2013, both have resumed sales of these products. One of the companies has switched to American poultry for its product,[77] while the other continues to produce jerky treats in China but has committed, through the settlement of a class action lawsuit by pet owners, to perform more testing of the ingredients and finished product it uses and to source poultry from just one supplier and one factory.[78]

Victims of tainted pet treats have been working to draw attention to this problem and demand action to prevent any more pets from falling ill. They have organized several petitions urging major pet food manufacturers to recall their products and are currently targeting retailers to urge them to stop selling pet treats imported from China. Recently Petco and Petsmart announced their intention to stop selling pet treats from China over the course of the next year,[79] and the Canadian pet food store chain, Global Pet Foods announced its intention to stop carrying pet treats made in China.[80]

Inadequate Labeling Requirements

One tool that U.S. consumers have is labeling, but in the case of both processed poultry products and pet treats, inadequate labeling rules leave consumers without all the information they need if they wish to avoid products from China.

Thanks to federal labeling requirements, country of origin labeling is required for beef, pork, lamb, chicken, goat meat, wild and farm-raised fish and shellfish, perishable agricultural commodities (fruits and vegetables), peanuts, pecans, ginseng, and macadamia nuts. But these labeling rules do not apply to processed forms of these foods, and the USDA's definition of processing is far too broad, which excludes many foods from the labeling requirement. This exemption includes processed forms of poultry that could soon be coming from Chinese plants.

Pet food and treats are not covered by country of origin labeling requirements that apply to human food. This makes it very difficult for consumers to know if these products were produced in or contain ingredients from China. The Customs Department oversees country of origin claims on products and relies on a standard that the country where a "substantial transformation" of raw materials into a finished product takes place is the country of origin. In the case of pet treats, the substantial transformation could indeed be the United States, resulting in a U.S.-origin label even if the product contains ingredients from China. There is no requirement for manufacturers list the country of origin for ingredients in their products.[81]

The Federal Trade Commission does regulate use of "Made in USA" labeling claims and relies on a standard that "major components" of a product must be of U.S. origin for a product to bear a "Made in USA" label.[82] But as the melamine-contamination of pet food illustrates, even minor ingredients that are adulterated can pose a health threat and, increasingly, these kinds of ingredients come from outside the United States.

<u>U.S. Policies to Address Unsafe Imports</u>

The World Trade Organization's Agreement on Agriculture has been a failure for farmers in the United States and has encouraged the growth of export platforms in places like China that benefit from low wages and weak regulatory standards, putting consumers around the world at risk. Congress and the Obama administration must revisit the current trade agenda to make public health, environmental standards and consumer safety the highest priorities when making decisions about trade policy. Specifically:

- The USDA should restart the process of determining if China's poultry inspection system is equivalent to the U.S. system and conduct an entirely new investigation before allowing Chinese poultry products to be exported to the United States.

- The USDA needs the resources to increase current levels of inspection of imported meat and poultry. If China is ever able to export processed poultry products from approved sources, USDA inspectors should be stationed in Chinese plants to ensure that Chinese-origin birds are not being processed into products destined for the United States.

- The FDA needs the resources to effectively inspect the growing volume of food imports from China and other countries. Congress and the Obama Administration must instruct and provide adequate funding for the FDA to increase import inspections, and to increase the rigor of those inspections to include testing for pathogens and chemical, pesticide and drug residues, and to increase inspection of processed food ingredients.

- The FDA needs the resources to conduct inspections in food facilities in China, rather than relying on third-party certifications of the safety practices used by exporting firms. The use of third-party certifications in China has already been shown to be questionable in the certifications used for organic products and in pilot projects on aquaculture conducted by the FDA. This type of system should not be used as a substitute for safety inspection by U.S. government inspectors.

- FDA should block the import of jerky pet treats from China until a cause of illnesses and deaths has been identified.

- FDA should require that any results that show contamination or adulteration of pet treats or ingredients from testing conducted by manufacturers be reported to the agency's Reportable Food Registry, as required by the FDA Food Safety Modernization Act.

- The USDA should close the loopholes in the current country of origin labeling rules and expand them to processed meats, fruits and vegetables. This labeling could be modeled on existing regulations for ground beef, which allow a "shotgun" label for products that may contain covered commodities from multiple sources.

- Congress should require mandatory country of origin labeling for foods not currently covered by existing law, to require basic manufacturing information about where, and by what company, processed foods were produced.

- For pet food and treats, FDA should work with the Customs Department and the Federal Trade Commission to develop labeling requirements that not only require disclosure of the country where the product was made, but also the origin of major ingredients, similar to how juice labeling provides the source of juice concentrate even if the product is reconstituted in the United States.

---

[1] U.S. Government Accountability Office (GAO). "Food Safety: FDA Can Better Oversee Food Imports by Assessing and Leveraging Other Countries' Oversight Resources." GAO-12-933. September 2012 at 1 and 5.
[2] Lohmar, Bryan et al. USDA ERS. "China's Ongoing Agricultural Modernization." EIB-51. April 2009 at 1.
[3] United Nations Food and Agriculture Organization (UN FAO). FAOStat. Country rank in the world, by commodity (quantity): China. Based on most recent data available, 2008. Available at http://faostat.fao.org/. Accessed December 14, 2010.
[4] Barboza, David. "U.S. Court Fines Chinese Vitamin C Makers." *New York Times.* March 15, 2013.

[5] "Mix of chemicals may be key to pet-food deaths." *CNN.* May 1, 2007; U.S. Government Accountability Office. "Food and Drug Administration Overseas Offices have Taken Steps to Help Ensure Import Safety, but More Long-Term Planning is Needed." GAO-10-960. September 2010 at 1.

[6] Barboza, David and Alexei Barrionuevo. "Filler in Animal Feed is Open Secret in China." *New York Times.* April 30, 2007; Barboza, David. "Discovery of Melamine-Tainted Milk Shuts Shanghai Dairy." *New York Times.* January 2, 2010.

[7] "Mix of chemicals may be key to pet-food deaths." *CNN.* May 1, 2007.

[8] Barboza, David. "An Export Boom Suddenly Facing a Quality Crisis." *New York Times.* May 18, 2007; USDA. Press release. "Joint Update: FDA/USDA Update on Tainted Animal Feed." Release No. 0121.07. March 2, 2007.

[9] Gale, Fred and Jean Buzby. USDA ERS. "Imports from China and food safety issues." Economic Information Bulletin No. 52. July 2009 at 10.

[10] U.S. Department of Agriculture Foreign Agricultural Service (USDA FAS). Global Agricultural Trade System (HS-10: 230100090, 2309100010.)

[11] U.S. Food and Drug Administration (FDA). Public Health Focus: Melamine Contamination in China. January 5, 2009. Available at http://www.fda.gov/NewsEvents/PublicHealthFocus/ucm179005.htm.

[12] Ee Lyn, Tan. "China eyes milk test after melamine deaths scandal." *Reuters.* June 15, 2010; Peterkin, Tom. "China milk scandal: 53,000 children fall ill from contaminated milk powder." *The (London) Telegraph.* September 22, 2008.

[13] Ee Lyn. June 15, 2010.

[14] "US Honey Makers Take a Swat at Chinese Smugglers." Andrew Schneider. AOL News. May 6 2010.

[15] Murphy, Joan. "Anti-dumping probe links large China shrimp exporter to transshipment." *Food Chemical News.* September 28, 2012.

[16] Food Sentry. Preliminary Analysis of International Food Safety Violations. Available at http://www.foodsentry.org/preliminary-analysis-of-international-food-safety-violations/. Accessed April 22, 2013.

[17] USDA FAS. Global Agricultural Trade System. Available at www.fas.usda.gov/gats/. (Food includes consumption imports of meat; fish & seafood; dairy; vegetables, fruits & nuts, coffee, tea & spices; cereals, oil seeds; fats; meat & fish preparations; sugar & confectionery; cocoa; cereal & dairy preparations; vegetable & fruit preparations; and miscellaneous edible preparations contained in two-digit harmonized codes: HS-2: 02, 03, 04, 07, 08, 09, 10, 11, 12, 15, 16, 17, 18, 19, 20, 21, 22.)

[18] Lee, Don. "China's additives on menu in U.S." *Los Angeles Times.* May 18, 2007.

[19] USDA FAS. Global Agricultural Trade System. (HS-10: 2912410000); Lee (2007).

[20] USDA FAS. Global Agricultural Trade System. (HS-6, 170490); Johnson, Tim. "China corners vitamin market." *Seattle Times.* June 3, 2007.

[21] USDA FAS. (HS-4, 1902 and 1905; HS-4, 2103; HS-10, 2309100090, 2039100010.)

[22] "Food safety situation still grim in China." *Associated Press.* March 3, 2009.

[23] "Chinese lawmakers call for enhancing supervision of food safety." *Xinhua.* February 25, 2010.

[24] "China Releases Five Year Food Safety Plan." *Food Safety News.* June 18, 2012.

[25] Barboza and Barrionuevo (2007).

[26] "96 arrested in China for selling adulterated milk powder." IANS. January 13 2011.

[27] FDA. Import Refusal Report Database. Refusal Actions by FDA as Recorded in OASIS for China. January 2011. Accessed March 2, 2011 with code 72BCT99.

[28] Olesen, Alexa. "China warns dairy producers inspectors watching for toxic melamine and leather protein in milk." *Associated Press.* February 17, 2011.

[29] Olesen, Alexa. "Skinny pigs, poison pork: China battles farm drugs." *Associated Press.* January 24, 2011.

[30] "China vows harsh penalties for food safety crimes." Associated Press. September 16, 2010.

[31] "62,000 illegal food cases in 11 months of 2011." Xinhua. January 10, 2012.

[32] Ramzy, Austin. "China Food Safety: Big Crackdown, but Big Concerns Remain." *Time.* August 5, 2011.

[33] McDonald, Mark. "From Milk to Peas, A Chinese Food-Safety Mess." *International Herald Tribune.* June 21, 2012.

[34] Martina, Michael and Sally Huang. "Chinese Police Bust Million-dollar Rat-meat Ring." *Reuters.* May 3, 2013.

[35] Barboza, David. "A Tide of Death, but This Time Food Supply Is Safe." *New York Times.* March 14, 2013.

[36] Yan, Wang. "Fake green peas latest food scandal." *China Daily,* China. March 31, 2010.

[37] "China media: Chinese liquor scandal." *BBC News*. November 22, 2012.
[38] Greenpeace. "Pesticides: Hidden Ingredients in Chinese Tea." 2012 at 1-2.
[39] Booth, Amy. "Residue concerns keep Chinese canned mushrooms off U.S. market." *Food Chemical News*. November 23, 2012.
[40] "Preserved fruit in China Tainted." *The New Paper*. April 30, 2012.
[41] "Chinese sellers accused of spraying cabbage with formaldehyde." Associated Press. May 7, 2012.
[42] Zuo, Mandy. "Dental cement used to calm fish" *South China Morning Post*. March 22, 2012.
[43] Wong, Edward. "Pollution Rising, Chinese Fear for Soil and Food." *New York Times*. December 30, 2013.
[44] Ibid.
[45] http://www.forbes.com/sites/kenrapoza/2014/02/05/no-end-in-sight-to-chinas-food-safety-woes/
[46] "Nearly 70% of Chinese Consumers Do Not Trust Food Safety." *Arirang News*. January 3, 2011.
[47] Gale and Buzby (2009) at 4.
[48] Wong. March 2, 2010.
[49] MacLeod, Calum. "China's organic farms rooted in food safety concerns." *USDA Today*. January 24, 2011.
[50] FDA. Import Refusal Database. Available at www.accessdata.fda.gov/scripts/importrefusals/. Accessed January-February 2011.
[51] FDA. Combined Field Activities – ORA. Program Activity Data. Field Foods Program Activity Data.
[52] Matsuda, Akane. "Food Safety Issues in the Vegetable Trade Between China and Japan: What Is Required to Establish Effective Food Safety Systems in the Bilateral Food Trade?" MPP Essay. Oregon State University, June 14, 2010.
[53] MacLeod, Calum. "China details new food-quality measures." *USA Today*. September 13, 2007.
[54] GAO (2010) at 12.
[55] Weisman, Steven. "China agrees to post U.S. safety officials in its food factories." *New York Times*. December 12, 2007; Zhe, Zhu. "U.S. food, drug agency opens Beijing office." *China Daily*. November 20, 2008.
[56] Lohmar, Bryan et al. USDA ERS. "China's Ongoing Agricultural Modernization." EIB-51. April 2009 at 24.
[57] Shames, Lisa. "Food Safety: FDA Could Strengthen Oversight of Imported Food by Improving Enforcement and Seeking Additional Authorities." GAO-10-699T. Testimony before the Subcommittee on Oversight and Investigations, U.S. House of Representatives Committee on Energy and Commerce. May 20, 2010 at 5.
[58] GAO. (2010) at 17.
[59] FDA. Combined Field Activities – ORA. Program Activity Data. Field Foods Program Activity Data.
[60] Quaid, Libby. "U.S. to allow processed poultry shipments from China." *Associated Press*. April 20, 2006; 71 Fed. Reg. 20867–20871.
[61] Quaid. April 20, 2006; "U.S. tries to sell beef to China amid food disputes." *Reuters*. June 29, 2007.
[62] USDA Food Safety and Inspection Service. "Final report of an initial equivalence audit carried out in China covering China's poultry inspection system." May 17 2005 at 9-11.
[63] Pub. L. 110-161. Title VII. §733.
[64] World Trade Organization. "United States—Certain Measures Affecting Imports of Poultry from China: Report of the Panel." WT/DS392/R. September 29, 2010 at 183-184.
[65] "China to levy anti-dumping duty on U.S. Poultry." *Bloomberg News*. September 26. 2010.
[66] Oliphant, James. "Obama and Hu Jintao pledge cooperation, downplay differences." *Los Angeles Times*. January 19, 2011
[67] Bottemiller, Helena. "USDA Petitioned to Block Chinese Poultry." *Food Safety News*. January 31, 2011.
[68] USDA Food Safety and Inspection Service. "Final Report of an Audit Conducted in the People's Republic of China." http://www.fsis.usda.gov/wps/wcm/connect/ed782de3-82e1-4298-aac9-14da84d1ebd2/2013_China_Poultry_Slaughter_FAR.pdf?MOD=AJPERES.
[69] Ibid.
[70] Siegel, Bettina Elias. "USDA Misinforms Parents Re: Chinese-Processed Chicken in School Meals." September 25, 2013. http://www.thelunchtray.com/usda-misinforms-parents-re-chinese-processed-chicken-in-school-meals/.
[71] Petition. "Congress: KEEP CHINESE CHICKEN OUT OF OUR SCHOOLS AND SUPERMARKETS!" http://www.change.org/petitions/congress-keep-chinese-chicken-out-of-our-schools-and-supermarkets

61

72 FDA. "FDA Investigates Animal Illnesses Linked to Jerky Pet Treats." September 14, 2012.
http://www.fda.gov/AnimalVeterinary/SafetyHealth/ProductSafetyInformation/ucm319463.htm
73 Aleccia, JoNel. "China stiff-arms FDA on jerky pet treat testing, reports show." NBCnews.com. August 22,
2012.
74 FDA. Recall—Firm Press Release. "Milo's Kitchen® Voluntarily Recalls Chicken Jerky and Chicken Grillers
Home-style Dog Treats." January 9, 2013.
75 FDA. "Questions and Answers Regarding Jerky Pet Treats." May 16, 2014.
http://www.fda.gov/AnimalVeterinary/SafetyHealth/ProductSafetyInformation/ucm295445.htm
76 Food Sentry. Press Release. "Global Food Monitoring Service Food Sentry Determines FDA May Be Looking
in the Wrong Place to Explain Toxicity of Chicken Jerky for Dogs." June 13, 2014.
http://www.digitaljournal.com/pr/1985981#ixzz34l7eeMHI
77 The VIN News Service. "Pet Treats: Does 'Made in USA' Mean Safe?" VIN News Service. June 10, 2014.
78 *Adkins v. Nestle Purina PetCare Co.* "Joint Motion for Preliminary Approval of Class Action Settlement,
Approval of Proposed Form of Notice, And Preliminary Certification of Settlement Class." May 30, 2014.
79 Lee, Jolie. "PetSmart, Petco to Stop Selling Dog and Cat Treats Made in China." *USA Today.* May 21, 2014.
80 Turnbull, Barbara. "Global Pet Foods Removes Chinese-produced Pet Treats from 160 Stores." TheStar.com.
June 12, 2014.
81 FDA. "Questions and Answers Regarding Jerky Pet Treats." May 16, 2014.
http://www.fda.gov/AnimalVeterinary/SafetyHealth/ProductSafetyInformation/ucm295445.htm.
82 U.S. Federal Trade Commission Bureau of Consumer Protection. "Complying with the Made in USA
Standard." http://www.business.ftc.gov/documents/bus03-complying-made-usa-
standard#Other%20Statutes.

———

PREPARED STATEMENT OF CHRISTOPHER J. D'URSO

JUNE 17, 2014

INTRODUCTION

According to President John F. Kennedy in his "Special Message to the Congress on Protecting the Consumer Interest", "If the consumer is unable to choose on an informed basis, then his dollar is wasted, his health and safety may be threatened, and the national interest suffers" (Kennedy). Unfortunately, this key tenet of consumer rights has been undermined by weak country of origin labeling (COOL) laws. Under the Tariff Act of 1930 and the Farm Bills of 2002 and 2008, imported products must be clearly labeled with country of origin. However, these laws contain a disturbing exemption which has been exploited and misconstrued by businesses: any imported product that is processed in the U.S. is not required to have COOL. Consequently, the majority of products remain unlabeled (Jurenas). As imports continue to increase, these inadequate laws not only compromise the consumer's right to know but also pose a threat to the public health and economy of the U.S. Thus, COOL must be required for all food products (defined as both human and pet), pharmaceuticals, and dietary supplements.

ISSUES WITH CURRENT COOL LAWS

The aforementioned COOL laws do not define what constitutes processing. Thus, U.S. Customs and Border Patrol, which enforces the Tariff Act for pharmaceuticals and dietary supplements, has broadly defined processing to be any method which results in the substantial transformation of a product whereby the product experiences a change in name, character, or use (Country of Origin Marking). On the other hand, the Agricultural Marketing Service (AMS), which enforces the Farm Bills for food products, has defined processing to be any type of cooking, curing, mixing, smoking, or restructuring (e.g. emulsifying and extruding). The interpretations of these agencies are highly subjective, loosely defined, and possibly contradictory. For instance, AMS has broadly construed their interpretation of processing to include mixing peas with carrots, roasting peanuts or pecans, and breading meat (Jurenas). Equally disturbing, chicken that is slaughtered in the U.S. can be exported to China for processing and subsequently re-exported to the U.S. as a nugget or soup without COOL (Strom). As a result of such loose standards, only 11% of pork, 30% of beef, 39% of chicken, and 40% of fruits and vegetables may be required to have COOL (Jurenas). The balances are either produced in the U.S. or imported and processed in the U.S. However, consumers will not know which is the reason. Therefore, Secretary of Agriculture Tom Vilsack has acknowledged that COOL exemptions "may be too broadly drafted" (qtd. in Jurenas).

IMPORTS TO THE U.S.

Compounding the issue of weak COOL laws, imports in pharmaceuticals, dietary supplements, and foods have reached all-time highs and are rapidly increasing. In the U.S. pharmaceutical industry, growth in the prescription drug market has flattened and the rate of return on pharmaceutical investments has dropped to just above the cost of capital. Coupled with demand for lower-cost products, these trends have caused a relocation of production to less developed nations such as China and India where the cost of formulation of an active pharmaceutical ingredient (API) can be 15–40% cheaper. Consequently, imports of pharmaceuticals increased by 13% annually from 2004 to 2011. Especially distressing, 10–15% of all food, including 60% of fruits and vegetables and 80% of seafood are imported (Pathway). As imports continue to rise so does the need for explicitly defining exemptions and strengthening COOL laws.

CONSUMERS' RIGHT TO KNOW

Weak COOL laws significantly undermine the right of consumers to be informed and make educated decisions. President Kennedy recognized this inalienable right as part of the Consumer Bill of Rights he presented in his Special Message to the Congress on Protecting the Consumer in 1962 (Kennedy). These rights were later codified in the United Nations Guidelines for Consumer Protection which affirm the consumer's right to "adequate information to enable them to make informed choices according to individual wishes and needs" (Guidelines). Without strong COOL laws, consumers are stripped of their right to know and thus their ability to avoid products from countries with poor quality or workmanship, inadequate safety regulations, human rights violations, or environmental concerns.

SAFETY AND PUBLIC HEALTH CONCERNS

Weak COOL laws place American public health at undue risk. According to the Food and Drug Administration (FDA), imports from developing countries such as China are increasing faster than imports from developed countries. Specifically, China is expected to see a 40% increase in exports by 2020 and 9% annual growth in food exports between 2010 and 2020 (Pathway). Unfortunately, China suffers from lower quality standards and compliance, lack of government oversight and regulation, and inadequate or inconsistent testing procedures. According to Dr. Peter Ben Embarek, food safety expert with the World Health Organization, "[Chinese food safety inspectors have] no clue what are the major food-borne diseases that need to be addressed or what are the major contaminants in the food process". Dr. Embarek elaborates that China uses a long-discredited method of randomly sampling and testing products (qtd. in LaFraniere). Furthermore, the U.S. Department of Agriculture notes that "refusals of food shipments from China suggest recurring problems with filth, unsafe additives . . . and veterinary drug residues" (Gale and Buzby).

Alarmingly, the FDA inspects only 1% of foreign shipments destined for the U.S. (Gale and Buzby). Equally distressing, the FDA admits that it "does not—nor will it—have the resources to adequately keep pace with the pressures of globalization". Specifically, it does not have sufficient resources to fully inspect foreign facilities, and it is impossible for them to meet the recommendations of the Government Accountability Office. In fact, the FDA has only inspected 1.5% of Chinese seafood processors selling to the U.S. At the current rate, it would take nine years for the FDA to inspect every high-priority, foreign pharmaceutical facility just once (Pathway).

Without FDA oversight and inspection, consumers are left vulnerable and are forced to protect themselves. This can be achieved through the use of COOL where consumers can avoid products from countries with known health and safety issues. Additionally, COOL provides traceability which may make it easier to address recalls and mitigate outbreaks of food-borne illnesses. For instance, COOL could have been implemented to combat the outbreak of mad cow disease in 2003–2005 since consumers would have had the information to avoid Canadian meat (Jurenas).

ECONOMIC IMPACT

Weak COOL laws may cause consumers to unknowingly purchase foreign products. Consequently, U.S. companies may lose business, American jobs may be eliminated, tax revenues may be reduced, dependency on imports may increase, and the U.S. trade imbalance may be exacerbated. On the other hand, U.S. companies will benefit from strengthened COOL laws since consumers will be more likely to purchase products labeled *Made in USA*. For example, a Florida Department of Agriculture and Consumer Services survey revealed 62% of consumers would purchase a product labeled *Made in USA* (VanSickle, et al.). As a result of the implementation of COOL in 2008, Canadian hog imports decreased 31% in the first year while Canadian and Mexican cattle imports decreased 10% each year from 2007 to 2009 (Jurenas).

Equally important, consumers may also be willing to pay a premium for products labeled *Made in USA*. In a study published by Colorado State University, 73% of consumers were willing to pay a 19% premium for ''USA Guaranteed'' steak and a 24% premium for ''USA Guaranteed'' ground beef due to safety concerns regarding imported beef, a strong desire to support U.S. producers, or beliefs that U.S. beef is of higher quality (Umberger, et al.). Based on these findings, the University of Florida estimated that implementing COOL would increase annual profits by $900 million for the U.S. steak industry and $3 billion for the U.S. ground beef industry (VanSickle, et al.). Similarly, in a study by The Boston Consulting Group, 80% of consumers were willing to pay 10–60% more for a variety of products labeled *Made in USA* even when imported products were cheaper (U.S. and Chinese Consumers). In another study published by Colorado State University, consumers were also willing to pay an increase in taxes of $183.77 per year to support mandatory COOL (Loureiro and Umberger). As a result of strong consumer preference for products labeled *Made in USA,* strengthened COOL laws will bestow undeniable benefits on American businesses and the economy.

INTERNATIONAL TRADE LAWS

Despite charges of protectionism, the World Trade Organization (WTO) has recently affirmed the right of countries to mandate COOL, especially for food products. Under Article IX of the General Agreement on Tariffs and Trade, WTO members are allowed to adopt laws requiring COOL to protect consumers (General Agreement). This provision was the subject of a WTO dispute in November 2009 when Canada and Mexico challenged U.S. COOL laws as unfairly discriminating against their products, causing their hog exports to the U.S. to decline (Jurenas). The Appellate Body ruled that mandatory COOL does not violate the Technical Barriers to Trade (TBT) Agreement. According to the Appellate Body, it did not matter if COOL laws ''have a detrimental impact on imports''. Instead, the determining factor is if COOL laws ''stem exclusively from a regulatory distinction rather than reflecting discrimination against the group of imported products''. Based on this reasoning, the Appellate Body ruled that U.S. COOL laws needed to be rewritten since ''COOL's recordkeeping and verification requirements . . . impose a burden on upstream producers and processors that is disproportionate to the level of origin information conveyed to consumers'' (qtd. in Ray and Schaffer). Originally, the labeling requirements at issue were weak since they did not require the disclosure of where the meat was born, raised, and slaughtered. As a result of this ruling, the U.S. was forced to enact stronger laws that required the explicit statement of where the aforementioned stages or steps occurred (Ray and Schaffer).

CONCLUSION

Incontrovertibly, weak COOL laws not only undermine consumer rights but also pose a threat to the U.S. public health and economy. Current laws do not require domestic products or imported products that are processed in the U.S. to have COOL. These exclusions have been too broadly construed to exempt the majority of imported foods, pharmaceuticals, and dietary supplements. As imports of these products continue to increase, strong COOL laws are vital now more than ever before. Strong COOL laws preserve consumer rights by enabling people to make informed purchasing decisions. Additionally, strong COOL laws safeguard the public health by allowing consumers to avoid potentially unsafe imports and by providing vital traceability. Furthermore, strong COOL laws will confer irrefutable benefits to American companies as a result of consumer preference and willingness to pay premiums for products labeled *Made in USA*. Despite charges of protectionism, the WTO has repeatedly affirmed the rights of countries to enforce COOL laws.

Unfortunately, the broad and inconsistent interpretations of exemptions to COOL laws increasingly affect my generation as the world becomes globalized, moving toward one market where supply chains are exceedingly complex. Moreover, my generation thrives on having immediate access to information so that we can express our preferences such as not purchasing products from countries with safety issues, human rights violations, or environmental concerns. Consequently, the processing exemption to mandatory COOL must be explicitly and objectively defined by law in order to eliminate loopholes, room for interpretation, and possible contradictions.

Equally important, all food products, pharmaceuticals, and dietary supplements, both foreign and domestic, must be required to have COOL.

WORKS CITED

"Country of Origin Marking." *Electronic Code of Federal Regulations.* U.S. Government Printing Office, n.d. Web. 2 Jun. 2014.

Gale, Fred and Jean C. Buzby. "Imports from China and Food Safety Issues." *Economic Research Service.* United States Department of Agriculture, Jul. 2009. Web. 2. Jun. 2014.

"General Agreement on Tariffs and Trade." World Trade Organization. *World Trade Organization,* Jul. 1986. Web. 14. Jul. 2013.

Jurenas, Remy. "Country-of-Origin Labeling for Food." *Congressional Research Service.* Library of Congress, 4 Jul. 2010. Web. 1 Jun. 2013.

Kennedy, John F. "Special Message to the Congress on Protecting the Consumer Interest." *The American Presidency Project.* The Regents of the University of California, n.d. Web. 19 Jul. 2013.

LaFraniere, Sharon. "In China, Fear of Fake Eggs and 'Recycled' Buns." *The New York Times.* The New York Times Company, 7 May 2011. Web. 14 Jul. 2013.

Loureiro, Maria, and Wendy Umberger. "Estimating Consumer Willingness to Pay for Country-of-Origin Labeling." *Journal of Agricultural and Resource Economics* 28.2 (2003): 287–301. Web. 1 Jun. 2013.

"Pathway to Global Product Safety and Quality." *U.S. Food and Drug Administration.* U.S. Department of Health and Human Services, 7 Jul. 2011. Web. 1 Jun. 2013.

Ray, Daryll, and Harwood Schaffer. "COOL Itself is Not Ruled Illegal by WTO but Finds Label Wording to Be a Problem." *Agricultural Policy Analysis Center.* The University of Tennessee, 22 Mar. 2013. Web. 19 Jul. 2013.

Strom, Stephanie. "Chinese Chicken Processors Are Cleared to Ship to U.S." *The New York Times.* The New York Times Company, 30 Aug. 2013. Web. 30 Aug. 2013.

Umberger, Wendy, et al. "Country-of-Origin Labeling of Beef Products: U.S. Consumers' Perceptions." *Journal of Food Distribution Research* 34.3 (2003): 103–116. Web. 1 Jun. 2013.

"United Nations Guidelines for Consumer Protection." *United Nations Sustainable Development Knowledge Platform.* United Nations, 2003. Web. 1 Jul. 2013.

"U.S. and Chinese Consumers Willing to Pay More for Made in USA Products." *The Boston Consulting Group.* The Boston Consulting Group, 15 Nov. 2012. Web. 19 Jul. 2013.

VanSickle, John, et al. "Country of Origin Labeling: A Legal and Economic Analysis." *Institute for Agriculture and Trade Policy.* Institute for Agriculture and Trade Policy, May 2003. Web. 1 Jun. 2013.

PREPARED STATEMENT OF HON. SHERROD BROWN, A U.S. SENATOR FROM OHIO; CHAIRMAN, CONGRESSIONAL-EXECUTIVE COMMISSION ON CHINA

JUNE 17, 2014

We have called this hearing to seek answers for American consumers, pet owners, farmers, and parents about the safety of pet treats, processed chicken, and animal feed from China.

Americans want to know where their foods come from and want to make sure that everything is being done to keep it safe.

Sixty-two million households in this country have a pet. They are raising 83 million dogs and 96 million cats just like members of their family.

That's why it's so troubling that seven years on, we still do not know what's causing the deaths and illnesses of thousands of dogs. Just last month, the FDA said that reports of illnesses had increased to 5,600 pets, including 1,000 dog deaths, and now three human illnesses. While no cause has been identified despite extensive study, the illnesses may be linked to pet treats from China.

Days later, major pet stores Petco and Petsmart announced they would be phasing out the sale of pet treats from China out of safety concerns.

Many of us still remember the pet food scare and recalls of 2007, the result of melamine-tainted pet food from China.

Given this, pet owners in Ohio and across America are rightfully concerned. When they go to the store to buy treats and food for their pet, they face difficult and confusing questions, just like the ones our family faces for our dog Franklin.

If something says it's made in China, can we be assured that it is safe? If it says it's made in the USA, what exactly does that mean? Is everything being done to keep pet treats safe?

Last year, the USDA declared that China is eligible to export processed, cooked chicken to the United States, paving the way for chicken sourced in the United States to be shipped to China for processing and then sold back to American consumers.

While no such chicken has entered our shores yet, it's possible that very soon this processed chicken could end up on our dinner tables and in our school lunchrooms.

Can we trust our Chinese counterparts to enforce safety up to our own standards, given China's poor enforcement of their own laws and rampant corruption? Will the label clearly indicate that the chicken was processed in China, so Americans can make an informed choice?

And finally, researchers are exploring a possible link between animal feed from China and the Porcine Epidemic Diarrhea Virus (PEDv) that has wiped out some 10 percent of our pig population. It's been a year and no definitive cause has been identified.

Americans want and require better answers, clearer labels, and the peace of mind that the foods we import from China are safe.

I appreciate the FDA and USDA being here to shed more light on these issues and to help American consumers better understand them.

In the meantime, I would urge the Chinese government to fully cooperate with our agencies and to make significant improvements in their food safety system.

And I would urge our FDA and USDA to continue devoting every effort to determining the cause of the pet illnesses and PEDv.

I urge companies to ensure the highest safety standards and to put pet and human safety first.

Finally, I would also urge us in Congress to consider whether we need to update our labeling requirements to take into account an increasingly globalized marketplace and to ensure the public health of our citizens.

PREPARED STATEMENT OF HON. CHRISTOPHER SMITH, A U.S. REPRESENTATIVE FROM NEW JERSEY; COCHAIRMAN, CONGRESSIONAL-EXECUTIVE COMMISSION ON CHINA

JUNE 17, 2014

Thank you very much, Chairman Brown. Thank you for calling this important hearing. I want to welcome our distinguished witnesses to this hearing on the important issue of the safety of our food products from China.

This is the second hearing on food safety that the Commission has done in the past year, and I especially want to thank Chairman Brown and our very dedicated and professional staff for their work to raise awareness about this issue, as well as all other human rights, rule of law, and governance issues.

The safety of food, feed, and drugs from China are a cause of real concern. American consumers are rightly anxious. We have pet treats that may have sickened and/or killed many pets across America. A virus may decimate 10 percent of American pigs, possibly from vitamins or feed from China. We have food products, including processed chicken, that may not have labeled as being made in China. In fact, it may have been labeled "Made in America."

I want to thank Chris D'Urso for bringing this last issue to my attention. The maze of labels and labeling requirements called Country of Origin Labeling makes it difficult for American consumers to make reasoned choices about the foods they eat and those foods that they feed to their pets.

Christopher D'Urso is one of the most outstanding young men that I have encountered. Not only did he achieve a perfect SAT score and ranked number one in his class, but his record of public service at such a young age is extraordinarily rare.

Last year we met and he brought information to me and to my staff, and to the Commission staff, about his research and findings regarding Origin of Labeling laws for the United States. The thoroughness and the level of understanding in such a complex and international issue was indeed impressive.

Having researched this issue since 2012, he pointed to the inadequacies of many of our current laws. In fact, consumers have the right to know the country of origin products, especially when they eat those products. I believe his future contributions will be significant.

On the issue of food safety, both Chinese and American consumers share serious concerns about food products made in China. I know I look, but again, we don't always know that what we're looking at is actually the truth. We really hope there can be more cooperation, accountability, and transparency in the future.

This past week was food safety awareness week in China. China's food industry has faced a real crisis of confidence over the past seven years. Despite government efforts, the number of scandals continue to grow: Meat that glows in the dark; exploding watermelons; 40 tons of bean sprouts containing antibiotics; rice contaminated with heavy metals; mushrooms soaked with bleach; and pork so filled with stimulants that athletes were told not to eat them, they would test positive for banned substances. All on top of the melamine-tainted milk powder that sickened some 300,000 children in 2007. As we all know, the World Health Organization [WHO] has said that melamine can cause kidney failure, bladder and kidney stones, and even may be a carcinogenic.

In response to that scandal, China passed its first ever food safety law. Nevertheless, we all know well that there is often a gap between what Chinese law says and what is enforced. China is still struggling to keep its food supply healthy.

The Chinese government is trying to crack down, we are told, recently closing some 5,000 food-producing businesses and arresting over 2,000 people. But experts on food safety say a needlessly complex bureaucracy and fierce determination to turn a profit means there will continue to be food safety scares and a Chinese public wary about its own supply.

While we think that this issue would have been solved already if China transferred resources to food safety from censoring the Internet and cracking down on free speech and political dissent, unfortunately, the government still seems to want safe pork but a silent public.

There is a direct connection between better human rights conditions in China and food safety. While China has had unprecedented economic growth for decades, it lags behind in ensuring the rights of its citizens and in developing transparency, official accountability and rule of law, things it certainly needs to tackle like the issue of food safety.

Transparency is absolutely necessary for any government to protect the health and well-being of citizens and to effectively manage problems related to food and drug safety. Remember the secrecy about the SAARS? Free speech and free press and freedom of association would allow crusading journalists in civil society to expose health scandals and work toward open solutions.

Those who try to skirt the law for profit would be exposed and citizens could work together with their government to ensure better and healthier food and water. A free press and muckraking journalists and novelists like Upton Sinclair—who we all recall wrote The Jungle about unsanitary meat, and it led to the Pure Food and Drug Act of 1906, that eventually morphed through legislation into the FDA—certainly helped to bring better food safety to the United States.

It may be tempting to say that China is on a learning curve that will eventually produce better food safety. But they need journalists, they need people who can speak out, use the Internet, and expose what is happening.

Let me conclude by saying U.S. trade policy must put health and safety of U.S. consumers and their pets as its top priority. Safety before profits is the message that has to be sent to producers, processors, and manufacturers.

If U.S. inspections are blocked or delayed for any reason, we should consider swiftly pulling products from shelves. In addition, the United States must tell authorities in China that they are held accountable for implementing and enforcing laws on food and drug safety.

The United States should be negotiating as part of its diplomatic relations better and smarter inspections, again, transparency in the food and drug supply chain, and closer collaboration between our food safety experts. Our labeling of food and feed products must be clear so that consumers know what they are buying and from whom, and where it comes from.

Last, the United States must continue to make human rights a top priority of U.S.-China relations, free speech, and an active civil society will do much more to ensure safer food and expose corruption.

I yield back, and I thank you.

Submission for the Record

Testimony Submitted for the Record by Terry Safranek, Representing Animal Parents Against Pet Treats Made In China

June 17, 2014

Chairman Brown, Co-Chairman Smith, and Members of the Commission. My name is Terry Safranek and I live in Brooklyn Heights, Ohio. I represent a group that I helped found called Animal Parents Against Pet Treats Made In China. We welcome this opportunity to make this statement today. We commend your leadership for holding this very important and timely hearing. I want to specifically thank Senator Brown for his dedication to this issue. I am so proud that he is my senator when I share with the group all of his actions, and how he has never given up or given in. They all call Senator Brown "Our Senator".

One month ago Petco and PetSmart—the nation's two largest specialty pet stores—announced that they would stop selling pet treats made in China. The announcement came on the heels of the FDA's latest report on victims of jerky from China. Unfortunately, this announcement came two and half years too late for my buddy Sampson.

In December of 2011, my little Sampson, a healthy, lively and hilarious fox terrier mutt was showing signs that he was not well. He seemed withdrawn, and his appetite was decreasing, and all he wanted was to drink water and urinate. His health rapidly decreased. We took him to the veterinarian 3 times in the next two weeks. Finally, blood tests revealed horrible results. Sampson was in acute renal failure. The Doc gave him intravenous fluids for 6 long, tormenting days. And then, the agonizing decision, the hardest, most heartbreaking decision. With my husband and children around us, I held my little buddy in my arms for the last time, as he was euthanized.

One day during this time, I saw a local family on the news, holding up a bag of Waggin' Train Chicken Jerky Treats! Their dog had eaten them died of renal failure a few weeks earlier, and their new little puppy was fed leftovers from the same bag—and became ill right away. As soon as they stopped the treats, he recovered. I was floored. It was the exact same treat that Sam had eaten; it had been his new favorite, and I was giving him them as a treat for about a month. I'm sure that was the only major change in his diet.

I went to the Waggin' Train comment boards, and there were hundreds of people furiously recounting their experience, begging for answers. Each of us was shocked to find we weren't alone, and the stories unmistakably similar. Shocked to find that the companies would accept no responsibility, even blamed US for overfeeding the treats! AS IF it's okay for a dog to be killed—by a treat!?

It was there that I met the pet parents of Bella, Ginger, Sophie, Heidi, Sarge, Shelbie and Annie, who would become my colleagues in this fight to protect other pets from this danger. Together we formed Animal Parents Against Pet Treats Made In China (APAPTMIC), a Facebook group, and a place for victims to gather, to share their stories, investigate the issue and make change.

Meeting all of these grieving pet parents made us realize how widespread the problem was. Each of these little ones suffered terribly, and we are devoted to being there to support their families, and help them to deal with the tragedy—and the overwhelming guilt at being a part of their senseless poisoning.

Together our little group began a journey that would lead us down many paths—in which we were complete novices. What we thought would be simple, turned into a herculean task. In our naivety we thought that the FDA would see all of these victims, with a clear connection to jerky from China and issue a recall. Nothing could be further from what actually happened.

Most disheartening of all, we learned that the warnings were there. Although the FDA has issued numerous cautions and alerts, they were unable to force a recall as they had not—still have not—identified the exact toxin. But is there a single toxin? Or is the issue a systemic one that is based in China? After all this time, and after ALL of the rigorous research, it is our conclusion that it is a systemic issue.

During these last two and a half years, we have watched the deaths associated with imported jerky treats climb to the current number of over 1000. 1000 deaths! More than one beloved pet was dying a horrible, painful death every single day in this country. Official figures indicate that 5,600 dogs, 24 cats, and 3 humans have become sick from contaminated jerky treats made in China. And how many thousands, tens of thousands, or more have gone unreported. How many have never made the connection?

We needed to raise awareness. We needed to figure out what we could do to STOP the senseless pet deaths caused by Chinese jerky. Not only has my group committed countless hours to research, we have rallied and lobbied for change that would bring about an end to the deaths and illnesses our pets have suffered because of these imported treats. Some of the actions we have taken include:

- Petitions targeting Nestle Purina, retailers and the FDA.
- Letter writing campaigns to manufacturers, retailers, veterinarians, media outlets and the FDA
- Became named plaintiffs in the nationwide Class Action lawsuits
- Attended and presented at Congresswoman DeLauro's Congressional Briefing on Chicken From China.
- Met with FDA representatives Tracey Forfa, Deputy Director of the Center for Veterinary Medicine and Sharon Natanblut, Senior Advisor for Strategic Communications and Public Engagement, FDA Office of Foods and Veterinary Medicine.

Although there had been no recall, we know that the FDA WAS making an effort. They weren't just publishing obscure warnings on their website. They enlisted the Veterinary Laboratory Investigation and Response Network (Vet-LIRN), the CVM, a network of veterinary labs and even NASA, but have yet to find a specific problem. We understand that many FDA officials were also genuinely frustrated. Bernadette Dunham, FDA's Director of the Center for Veterinary Medicine, refers to the investigation as "One of the most elusive and mysterious outbreaks we've encountered".

In January 2013, the New York State Department of Agriculture & Markets (NYSDAM) found illegal antibiotic residue on the treats. This caused a "voluntary withdrawal" of three of the most consumed and most complained about brands: Nestle Purina's Waggin' Train and Canyon Creek Ranch (all varieties) and Del Monte's Milo's Kitchen (2 varieties). We were cheered to know that, at long last the deaths and illnesses being reported to the FDA would decrease substantially. But it was still hard to understand why the FDA wasn't more aggressive, when there is clearly a link of jerky treats to pet illnesses. The anecdotal evidence seems overwhelming.

We decided to tackle the problem that each and every victim we knew had faced: if only I had known what the FDA knew! Our dogs were dead or suffering chronic illness because we didn't know there was a problem.

Perhaps the most important of our actions is the petition asking the FDA to implement Section 211 of the Food Safety Modernization Act (FSMA), called FDA: POST CONSUMER NOTICES WHERE WE CAN SEE THEM. The FDA has always claimed their hands are tied when it comes to warning consumers about reported products at the point of sale, but this is no longer true. In 2011, Congress finally enacted the Food Safety Modernization Act (FSMA) which explicitly gives the FDA this authority. But of course, it is never that simple. Ever since that time, the law—which encompasses all food, for pets or humans—was sitting in of the Office of Management and Budget waiting for review.

With just a simple piece of paper posted on store shelves, millions of American families can be spared the consequences of purchasing potentially dangerous products. We believe that the FDA has the responsibility to inform consumers of possible risks and we have the RIGHT to make informed decisions. A trip to the grocery store should not be deadly!

We strongly believe that Section 211 of the FSMA needs to be implemented as quickly as possible. If only we would have been warned at point of sale, we might have been spared the many, many tears we have shed, grieving our lost dogs.

Imagine our devastation when it was announced in March of 2014 that Nestle Purina was returning Waggin' Train—the most reported brand associated with complaints of illness and death, to the market. The product is STILL MADE IN CHINA. From the Waggin' Train website Q & A: "As we said back in January 2013, we planned to re-introduce products once we determined the best way to address the regulatory inconsistencies between countries that led to the voluntary withdrawal." What does that even mean? Did they simply get the rules changed? This is truly frightening.

If we have learned anything, it is that consumers desperately need the protection of the US government against these multi-national mega-corporations, whose ultimate loyalty is to profit. As consumers, we don't stand a chance without the weight of the government behind us.

Since April of 2012, several nationwide class action lawsuits have been working their way through the courts. The first, largest and most visible is Adkins v. Nestle

Purina PetCare Co. Two years later, an agreement was reached. Nestle Purina PetCare Co. agreed to create a $6.5 million settlement fund to compensate dog owners who claim that their animals were harmed by their jerky treats from China. As of this writing, this agreement has not yet been finalized, awaiting approval of the Court.

The Quality Assurance and Quality Control stipulations in the agreement are a crucial part of the agreement. Enhanced labeling and testing, and holding these companies accountable for the health and safety of their customers is the goal. But all of this is just a small piece of a huge puzzle.

In our stores and across the country, people are waking up to the risks of chicken from China. But not enough have the knowledge that they require to make an educated choice. This is why we are so passionate about strengthening the FDA and the FSMA. There are too many loopholes that allow hazards to reach our homes and families. This is our last line of defense!

It seems that government rules and regulations are endless, so we are concentrating on the few that we feel would have avoided such needless suffering:

- IMPLEMENT FSMA SECTION 211 requiring warnings to be prominently displayed in stores;
- AMEND FSMA SECTION 211 to include all retailers, not just major chains;
- SPECIFY THAT WRITTEN WARNINGS must be displayed with the affected product, not just at the cash register;
- EMPOWER the FDA to force a recall if there is a reasonable probability that an article of food is adulterated;
- INCLUDE classes of products that have been identified by the FDA to be injurious to human and/or animal health. If the FDA is issuing advisories, cautions and warnings to customers on their website, then we strongly believe that such information should be broadcast as widely as possible. The Chinese pet treats are a perfect example of such a class of product.

For myself, and on behalf of Animal Parents against Pet Treats Made in China, I want to sincerely thank The Congressional-Executive Commission on China for the important work you are doing, and allowing us to submit this statement. As a regular consumer, it's easy to get discouraged and start to feel hopeless and helpless. Then my spirit is renewed to know that we do have great representatives who are just as dedicated, and are ceaselessly working behind the scenes on our behalf.

Terry Safranek, Brooklyn Heights, Ohio
Tracey Bagatta, Center Moriches, NY
Robin Pierre, Pine Bush, NY
Kaly White, Akwesasne NY
Steve Poponick, Latrobe, PA
Raymond Parker, Knoxville, TN

QUESTIONS AND ANSWERS FOR THE RECORD

QUESTIONS FOR CVM DEPUTY DIRECTOR, TRACEY FORFA, J.D. FROM CHAIRMAN BROWN

Question. We understand that FDA has plans to increase its U.S. staff in China from 8 to 27 staff.

Is 27 enough to ensure the safety of regulated food and drugs from China and if so how did FDA make this determination? Will this lead to an increase in food and drug inspections and by how much?

Answer. The Food and Drug Administration's (FDA or the Agency) plan to increase staffing in the China office to 27 represents more than a three-fold increase. FDA is optimistic that the increased staffing will expand the Agency's capacity to detect and address risks for foods, drugs, and ingredients manufactured in China that are exported to the United States. It will enhance FDA's ability to ensure that Chinese manufacturers, processors, packers, and distributors institute measures to assure that foods, drugs, and ingredients imported into the United States are safe and meet FDA standards. At full staff, the Agency expects the number of food and drug inspections by in-country staff to increase by about 200 inspections annually. FDA expects to further assess the sufficiency of our capacity once the planned increases in staffing are in place.

Until new staff members are brought in to the FDA China Office, FDA will continue to staff the office as well as conduct inspections in China through short-term trips made by FDA consumer safety officers (CSOs) based in the United States. This is in addition to our ongoing measures to ensure the safety of products offered for importation into the United States from China and other countries. For example, FDA electronically screens all imports using an automated risk-based system to determine if shipments meet identified criteria for physical examination or other review. FDA developed the Predictive Risk-based Evaluation for Dynamic Import Compliance Targeting application, or PREDICT, to enhance the Agency's ability to target high-risk products. This sophisticated screening system uses information from many sources—such as intrinsic product risks, past inspection results, intelligence data, and information about such threats as extreme weather that could spoil a shipment—to provide the entry reviewer with risk scores on every import line. This system allows FDA to focus its resources on those imports that are most likely to pose a danger.

Question. Of the 19 new staff, have all of them received their visas and if not, why not?

Answer. FDA is working to complete the hiring process for new staff for the China Office and is actively recruiting and interviewing staff to fill vacancies in the inspectorate, food policy, and supervisory staff there. The Agency expects to begin submitting several more visa applications in FY 2015.

There are currently two visa applications pending with the Chinese Government for staff members who were hired for the FDA China Office in FY 2012 and FY 2013. In discussions connected with the December 2013 visit to Beijing by Vice President Joe Biden, the Chinese Government assured FDA that it would begin granting visas for an increased number of U.S. food and drug CSOs stationed in China.

Question. How many of the 19 new staff have already taken up their positions in China?

Answer. As we indicated in our answer to the previous question, FDA is working to complete the hiring process for new staff for the China Office and is actively recruiting and interviewing staff to fill vacancies there.

Question. Has the FDA faced any delays or other problems in obtaining visas for U.S. staff to go to China in 2014? If so, please describe the delays or other problems and what steps FDA is taking to address the issue?

Answer. Since October 2012, there have been five visas delayed. Three of the FDA staff members who were waiting for visa approval have decided to pursue opportunities in other parts of the Agency, so there are currently two visas that are pending.

As we stated in our response to Question 2, in addition to the two visas currently pending, FDA expects to begin submitting several more visa applications in FY 2015.

QUESTION FOR CVM DEPUTY DIRECTOR, TRACEY FORFA, J.D. FROM COCHAIRMAN SMITH

Question. Just on the visa delay, how many visas have been delayed or denied?

Answer. Since October 2012, there have been five visas delayed. Three of the Food and Drug Administration (FDA or the Agency) staff members who were waiting for visa approval have decided to pursue opportunities in other parts of the Agency, so there are currently two visas that are pending. In the meantime, the FDA has been supplementing its China staff with FDA investigators on short-term (60-, 90-, or 120-day) assignments. Many of the FDA investigators who have done short-term assignments in China over the last two years are now applying to be posted in China for long-term assignments.

In discussions connected with the December 2013 visit to Beijing by Vice President Joe Biden, the Chinese Government assured FDA that it would begin granting visas for an increased number of U.S. food and drug consumer safety officers (CSOs) stationed in China.

ADDITIONAL QUESTION FOR THE RECORD FOR CVM DEPUTY DIRECTOR, TRACEY FORFA, J.D. FROM CHAIRMAN BROWN

Question. Do you know enough about the larger system to be able to say definitively that all of these ingredients [in Happy Hips treats which bear the label, "Made in the USA"] are from the United States?

Answer. As an initial matter, the product may be subject to labeling requirements imposed by the Department of Homeland Security's Customs & Border Protection (CBP). CBP has responsibility for implementing country-of-origin labeling requirements on certain food articles, including pet food. CBP requires country-of-origin labeling—they call it "marking"—on imported, foreign-origin food articles or their containers unless there is a "substantial transformation" of the food in the United States before it is distributed to the public. It is also my understanding that, in general, the origin of individual ingredients in a food product is not required to be marked on the food product if the ingredient undergoes substantial transformation in the manufacture of the food product.

Even if CBP determines that, due to substantial transformation in the U.S., an imported ingredient in a food product does not need a foreign country-of-origin mark, it still might not be permissible to label the food product as "Made in the USA" if it has foreign ingredients. Under the Federal Food, Drug, and Cosmetic Act, a food is misbranded if its labeling is false or misleading. The Food and Drug Administration (FDA) would make such a determination regarding a "Made in the USA" statement on a label on a case-by-case basis, consulting as appropriate with CBP and the Federal Trade Commission, which regulates "Made in the USA" claims in advertising.

FDA food labeling regulations also require that the label of a packaged food, including pet food, bear the name and place of business of the manufacturer, packer, or distributor. The statement of place of business must contain the street address (unless the firm's name and address are listed in a current city directory or telephone book); city or town; state (or country, if outside the United States); and zip code (or mailing code used in countries other than the United States). While there is no requirement that the label specifically identify the name and address of the food manufacturer, if the firm identified on the label is not the manufacturer of the food, the firm name must be accompanied by a qualifying phrase that states the firm's relationship to the product, e.g., "manufactured for" or "distributed by." If an individual has questions about the country of origin of a particular product or its ingredients, that person may contact the company on the label to request information.